NEW YORK REVIEW BOOKS
CLASSICS

T0022903

GRIEF LESSONS

EURIPIDES (c. 484–c. 406 BC), generally believed to have
been born into a prominent family from northern Attica, was
the author of some ninety plays, eighteen of which survive to
this day. Starting in 455 BC, he competed in twenty-two of the
annual Athenian dramatic competitions and won the first prize
five times. Ridiculed in the comedies of his contemporary
Aristophanes, Euripides left Athens late in life for the court
of King Archelaus of Macedonia. Otherwise almost nothing
is known of the life of the writer whom Aristotle called "the
most tragic of tragedians."

ANNE CARSON teaches at the University of Michigan.
Among her books are *Eros the Bittersweet, Autobiography of
Red, If Not, Winter: Fragments of Sappho,* and *Decreation.*

GRIEF LESSONS
FOUR PLAYS

EURIPIDES

Translated by
ANNE CARSON

NEW YORK REVIEW BOOKS

New York

THIS IS A NEW YORK REVIEW BOOK
PUBLISHED BY THE NEW YORK REVIEW OF BOOKS
435 Hudson Street, New York, NY 10014
www.nyrb.com

The Library of Congress has cataloged the hardcover edition as follows:

Euripides.
  [Selections. English. 2006]
  Grief lessons : four plays by Euripides / by Euripides ; translated and with an introduc-
tion by Anne Carson.
    p. cm.
  ISBN 1-59017-180-2 (alk. paper)
  1. Euripides—Criticism and interpretation. I. Carson, Anne. II. Title.
PA3975.A2 2006
822'.01—dc22

                         2006009092

ISBN 978-1-59017-253-7

Printed in the United States of America on acid-free paper.
10 9 8

Contents

NOTE

Numbers in the margins refer to the lines of the
present translation; numbers at the top right of
the pages to the lines of the original Greek text.

PREFACE

Tragedy: A Curious Art Form

Why does tragedy exist? Because you are full of rage. Why are you full of rage? Because you are full of grief. Ask a headhunter why he cuts off human heads. He'll say that rage impels him and rage is born of grief. The act of severing and tossing away the victim's head enables him to throw away the anger of all his bereavements.[1] Perhaps you think this does not apply to you. Yet you recall the day your wife, driving you to your mother's funeral, turned left instead of right at the intersection and you had to scream at her so loud other drivers turned to look. When you tore off her head and threw it out the window they nodded, changed gears, drove away.

Grief and rage—you need to contain that, to put a frame around it, where it can play itself out without you or your kin having to die. There is a theory that watching unbearable stories about other people lost in grief and rage is good for you—may cleanse you of your darkness. Do you want to go down to the pits of yourself all alone? Not much. What if an actor could do it for you? Isn't that why they are called actors? They act for you. You sacrifice them to action. And this sacrifice is a mode of deepest intimacy of you with your own life. Within it you watch [yourself] act out the present or possible organization of your nature. You can be aware of your own awareness of this nature as you never are at the moment of experience. The actor, by reiterating you, sacrifices a moment of his own life in order to give you a story of yours.

1. Renato Rosaldo, "Grief and the Headhunter's Rage," *Text, Play, and Story*, edited by E. M. Bruner (Washington, D.C.: American Ethnological Society, 1984), pp. 178–195.

Curious art form, curious artist. Who was Euripides? The best short answer I've found to this is an essay by B. M. W. Knox, who says of Euripides what the Corinthians (in Thucydides) said of the Athenians, "that he was born never to live in peace with himself and to prevent the rest of mankind from doing so." Knox's essay is called "Euripides: The Poet As Prophet."[2] To be a prophet, Knox emphasizes, requires living in and looking at the present, at what is really going on around you. Out of the present the future is formed. The prophet needs a clear, dry, unshy eye that can stand aloof from explanation and comfort. Neither will be of interest to the future.

One thing that was really going on for much of Euripides' lifetime was war—relatively speaking, world war. The Peloponnesian War began 431 BC and lasted beyond Euripides' death. It brought corruption, distortion, decay and despair to society and to individual hearts. He used myths and legends connected with the Trojan War to refract his observations of this woe. Not all his plays are war plays. He was also concerned with people as people—with what it's like to be a human being in a family, in a fantasy, in a longing, in a mistake. For this exploration too he used ancient myth as a lens. Myths are stories about people who become too big for their lives temporarily, so that they crash into other lives or brush against gods. In crisis their souls are visible. To be present when that happens is Euripides' playwriting technique. His mood, as Walter Benjamin said of Proust's, is "a perfect chemical curiosity."[3]

There is in Euripides some kind of learning that is always at the boiling point. It breaks experiences open and they waste

2. *Directions in Euripidean Criticism: A Collection of Essays*, edited by Peter Burian (Duke University Press, 1985), pp. 1–12.
3. Walter Benjamin, "The Image of Proust," *Illuminations*, edited by Hannah Arendt, translated by Harry Zohn (Schocken, 1968), pp. 203–204.

themselves, run through your fingers. Phrases don't catch them, theories don't hold them, they have no use. It is a theater of sacrifice in the true sense. Violence occurs; through violence we are intimate with some characters onstage in an exorbitant way for a brief time; that's all it is.

HERAKLES

PREFACE

Q: Will you admit this fact, that we are at a turning point?
A: If it's a fact it's not a turning point.[1]

Herakles is a two-part man. Euripides wrote for him a two-part play. It breaks down in the middle and starts over again as does he. Wrecks and recharges its own form as he wrecks and recharges his own legend. Two-part: son of both Zeus (god) and Amphitryon (man) he is immortal, *maybe*—experts disagree and he himself is not sure. Container of uncontainable physical strength, he civilizes the world by vanquishing its monsters then returns home to annihilate his own wife and children. Herakles is a creature whose relation to time is a mess: if you *might* be immortal you live in all time and no time at the same time. You end up older than your own father and more helpless than your own children. Herakles is a creature whose relation to virtue is a mess: human virtue derives from human limitation and he seems to have none; gods' virtue does not exist. Euripides places him in the midst of an awareness of all this. But awareness for Herakles is no mental event, it comes through flesh.

Herakles' flesh is a cliché. Perfect physical specimen, he cannot be beaten by any warrior, by any athlete, by any monster on the earth or under it. The question whether he can be beaten even by death remains open; it is a fact that he has gone down to Hades and come back alive: here is where the play starts. This fact becomes the turning point—the overturning point—of his cliché.

1. Maurice Blanchot, interview with himself, *La Nouvelle Revue Française*, April 1960.

How do you overturn a cliché? From inside. The first eight hundred lines of the play will bore you, they're supposed to. Euripides assembles every stereotype of a Desperate Domestic Situation and a Timely Hero's Return in order to place you at the very heart of Herakles' dilemma, which is also Euripides' dilemma: Herakles has reached the boundary of his own myth, he has come to the end of his interestingness. Now that he's finished harrowing hell, will he settle back on the recliner and watch TV for the rest of time? From Euripides' point of view, a playwright's point of view, the dilemma is practical. A man who can't die is no tragic hero. Immortality, even probable immortality, disqualifies you from playing that role. (Gods, to their eternal chagrin, are comic). For this practical dilemma Euripides' solution is simple. From inside the cliché he lets Herakles wreck not only his house, his family, his perfection, his natural past, his supernatural future, but also the tragedy itself. Into the first half of the play he packs an entire dramatic *praxis*, complete with reversals, recognitions, laments, revenge, rejoicing, suspense and death. This melodrama ends at 814. The actors leave the stage. You may think it's over and head for the door.

But if you stay you will see Herakles pull the whole house of this play down around himself, tragic conventions and all. Then from inside his *berserker furor* he has to build something absolutely new. New self, new name for the father, new definition of God. The old ones have stopped. It is as if the world broke off. Why did it break off? Because the myth ended. If you pay attention to the chorus—especially their last utterance which is very, very brief—you will hear them make a strange remark. After the murder by Herakles of his own family they respond (992ff/1020ff)*:

*Please note that the first set of figures given refers to the line numbers of the present translation, the second to those of the Greek text.

... these evils here
belonging to the son of Zeus
go far beyond
anything in the past.

. . . .

What groaning,
what lament,
what song of death,
what dance of Hades
shall I do?

The Greek word *choros* means a dance accompanied by song, also the people who perform the dance. One of the functions of the tragic chorus is to reflect on the action of the play and try to assign it some meaning. They typically turn to the past in their search for the meaning of the present—scanning history and myth for a precedent. It was Homer who suggested we stand in time with our backs to the future, face to the past. What if a man turns around? Then the chorus will necessarily fall silent. This story has not happened before. Notice they do not dance again. Let the future begin.

As we look back from the future at this old tragedy and its (all too contemporary) brutalized and brutalizing hero, we might consider some aspects of the play and its production that are foreign to modern tastes or expectation. Nowadays we think of a play as something that happens inside a small black box with artificial lighting. The ancient theater of Dionysos at Athens could seat 12,000 to 15,000 spectators and its plays were performed in daylight, starting at dawn. The backdrop of the theatrical space (the space in a modern theater that appears when the curtains part) was formed by open air. At Athens the audience looked out on miles and miles of Aegean Sea. No curtain, very little set. Closest to the audience was a round *orchestra* ("dancing space") where the chorus performed its songs and dances; behind this, a stage building of some kind (e.g. Herakles' house) where the actors went in and out. Two *parodoi* ("side roads") permitted entrances and exits from the wings. The play's action was performed in the small area between the *orchestra* and the stage building. Violence was not presented onstage. Violent acts and death were at times audible while happening inside the stage building or narrated afterwards by an eyewitness (usually the Messenger). Occasionally the consequences of violent acts that had taken place inside were extruded onto the stage on a mechanism called the *ekkyklema* ("rolling platform") e.g. the mayhem visited by Herakles upon his family. Think tableau. In a theater of such scale, much of the audience's visual experience would have been an appreciation of tableau—a design of bodies moving or posed in space a long distance away. Hence the conceptual importance and symbolic possibilities of posture: you can read the plot of a play off the sequence of postures assumed by its characters. Up is winning, down is losing, bent is inbetween. Herakles' unlucky family is shown at first semi-prostrate on the stage in supplication for their lives, then briefly upright while Herakles champions them, then strewn as corpses. Herakles himself enters gloriously upright but is soon reduced to a huddled and broken form. His task in the last third of the play is to rise from this prostration, which he does with the help of Theseus. Euripides makes clear that Herakles exits at the end leaning on his friend. Herakles' reputation in myth and legend otherwise had been that of lonehand hero. Here begins a new Heraklean posture. Meanwhile throughout the play this image of collaborative heroism is embodied, movingly, in the tableau of the chorus. They are old men; they lean on sticks or on each other. All mortals come to this.[2]

Gods remain a problem. You will hear gods' names and see their consequences rawly displayed throughout the speeches and the action. You will sympathize with the chorus who cower before them and also with Herakles who decides not to believe in them —not to believe, that is, in *the story of his own life*. Bold move. Perhaps he is a tragic hero after all.

2. Herakles also figured for the Greeks as a symbol of eternal youth; according to legend he ascended to Mount Olympos after death, married the goddess Hebe (Youth) and lived forever. Euripides does not introduce this strand of the myth directly for he wants to tell the story of a mortal man or at least one whose magic fails him. Yet youth and age are thematically present in every choral ode and also in certain striking mimetic gestures of the play: the rock-like weight of old age of which the chorus complain at 619/638 is realized in the rock that Athene hurls at Herakles to check his frenzy (976–979/1003–1006; cf. 1380/1397); the veil of shadow that old age feels upon its eyes at 620/641 is realized in the shadowy covering that Herakles draws over his head at the approach of Theseus (1137/1159; 1206/1216); Herakles takes Theseus as son (1384/1401) and looks forward to burying his own father (1406/1421). Time is uneasy in this play and it unsettles the cliché of heroic autonomy.

CAST OF CHARACTERS

In order of appearance

AMPHITRYON (MORTAL), *father of Herakles*
MEGARA, *wife of Herakles*
three SONS *of Herakles and Megara*
CHORUS *of old men of Thebes*
LYKOS, *usurper of Thebes*
SERVANTS *of Lykos*
HERAKLES, *son of Zeus/Amphitryon and of Alkmene*
IRIS, *messenger of the gods*
MADNESS
THESEUS, *king of Athens*
MESSENGER

The scene is set at Thebes. The stage has two side entrances and a central stage building representing the house of Herakles. Nearby is an altar of Zeus Savior where Amphitryon, Megara and the children sit as suppliants.

AMPHITRYON

Who does not know the man who shared his marriage bed
with Zeus?
Amphitryon,
son of Alkaios,
grandson of Perseus,
father of Herakles,
me!
I used to own Thebes,
where dragons' teeth sprang out of the earth like ears of corn
and lived as men.   10
Their children fill this city.
From them came Kreon, ruler of this land
and father of Megara—
wedding songs rang out
when Herakles led her to my home as his bride.
But he left Thebes behind,
left Megara, left me—
to live in that Argive city
from which I was exiled
because I committed a murder.   20
He wanted to dwell there, to ease my way back.
The price was high:

to civilize the entire world was his contract.
I wonder, did Hera have her spike in him then
or was it all just his fate?
Anyway, the task is finished now
except one last labor—
the threebodied dog must be got up from hell.
He went down there but has not come back.

According to legend   30
Dirke's husband long ago was Lykos,
despot of this sevengated city.
And it is his grandson, with the same name,
who came from Euboia, murdered Kreon and rules us now.
The city was divided, he fell upon it.
Then our kinship with Kreon turned out a bad thing.
And now that my son is down in the basement of the world,
glorious Lykos wants us dead—Herakles' children,
Herakles' wife (to quench the seed)
and me, the man of the family I guess,   40
though I'm useless and old.
Blood justice is what Lykos fears.

So I—left in the house here
to care for the children, along with their mother,
when my son went underground—
I've set us up at the altar of Zeus Savior,
built by my son to mark his victory
over the Minyans.
Here we watch and wait,
lacking everything—food, water, clothing,   50
on the bare ground,
sealed out of our house.

Who can help?
Friends disappear
or they are powerless.
This is what misfortune means
an acid test of friendship.
I wouldn't wish it on anyone.

MEGARA

Old man—you who once demolished the Taphians' city,
you who commanded an army for Thebes—   60
nothing the gods do makes sense!
I was no outcast from luck on my father's side.
He was rich and big and boasted
of his power, long spears leaping around it,
boasted of his children.
He gave me to your son,
to Herakles, a brilliant marriage.
And now all that has vanished.
You and I will die, old man,
and Herakles' little fledglings—   70
like a bird I cover them with my wings.
They fly to me asking one after another,
Where is father gone?
What is he doing?
When will he come back?
I put them off with stories.
It shocks me,
whenever the doors creak everyone jumps up
as if to run to their father's knee.
Can you ease me with hope or some way of salvation, old man? 80
I look to you.
We could never cross the border secretly,

guards are posted on every road.
Nor can we hope for salvation from friends anymore.
Whatever your thoughts,
speak them. Death is at hand.

AMPHITRYON

Daughter, I find it hard
to rattle off advice like that.
We're weak, let's play for time.

MEGARA

Wait for worse? You love the light so much? 90

AMPHITRYON

I do, I love its hopes.

MEGARA

Well yes, but there's no use expecting the impossible, old man.

AMPHITRYON

To delay evils is a kind of cure.

MEGARA

This waiting gnaws at me.

AMPHITYON

A clear path may open
out of these troubles, for you and me.
My son might come.
Be calm. Wipe their tears
and soothe them with stories,
a bit of make-believe. 100

Even catastrophes grow weary,
no wind can keep blasting all the time.
And great happiness in the end falters.
Yes, all is change.
Best to keep hoping.
Despair is the mark of a bad man.

[enter Chorus from both side entrances into orchestra]

CHORUS (*entrance song*)
Leaning on my stick I come,
   quavering my laments,
      like some old white bird—
         I am nothing but words,   110
            just a shape
               of dreams or night.
         I tremble. But my heart is full!
      O poor fatherless children,
   poor old man,
  poor mother calling out
to your husband in Hades.

Come do not tire, heavy foot, heavy leg,
   heavy burden, uphill
      like a workhorse   120
        I go.
           Take my hand,
       take my robe,
     where the foot falters.
    Old man side by side with old man—
  as our young spears once stood side by side in war,
no shame to our glorious country.

Look how the gorgon-gaze of their father
stares out of their eyes.
Bad luck is not gone from these children,   130
but neither is beauty.
O Greece! what fighters you will lose
when you lose these!

But I see Lykos coming.
Lykos, tyrant of this land.

[enter Lykos by side entrance with Servants]

LYKOS

You people!—Herakles' people,
if I may, a question:
and since I am master here,
yes! you must answer.
How long do you think to prolong life?   140
What hope do you have? What defense do you see?
Or do you believe
he will come back from Hades?
Hysteria!
You, boasting you sowed the same marriage bed as Zeus,
and you, that you married a world hero!
What was so spectacular about those "labors" of his anyway?
So he killed a water snake, or that Nemean creature—
he did it with nets, not his own hands.
Is this your claim? Is this why you think   150
his sons should escape death?
A man who got a name for courage,
though he was *nothing*—he fought animals!
No good for anything else.

Never had a shield on his arm,
never came near a spear: he used a bow!—
coward's weapon—always ready to run.
A bow is no test of a man's courage.
No—but standing fast, staring the enemy down,
facing the gash of the spear!   160
Now me,
I'm not shameless,
just cautious, old man.
I killed Kreon, her father,
I know that. I sit on his throne.
Don't want those boys
reared up as avengers on me.

AMPHITRYON
Let Zeus defend the Zeus-part of his son.
The rest is mine: Herakles,
I'll show this man knows nothing about you.   170
To hear you abused—no!
Against unspeakable charges, like cowardice,
I call the gods to witness.
I call the lightning of Zeus, the chariot of Zeus,
in which you went to shoot the giants down
and raised a cry of victory with the gods.
Go to where the centaurs live, ask them—
those monsters on four legs—ask
what man they judge the bravest: they'll say
my son!   180
Whereas, if you ask Dirphys, your own local mountain,
to praise you, she couldn't name a single deed of yours.
And then you denounce that tactical masterpiece,
the bow.

27

Listen, you'll learn something.
Your hoplite is the slave of his weapons.
If he breaks his spear he's dead.
Dead too if his comrades on either side aren't good men.
But the one who aims a bow—
world's best weapon—can shoot a thousand arrows   190
and still have some to save his life.
He stands back, wounds his enemy with invisible shots
and keeps his own body
unexposed. This is intelligent warfare,
to damage the enemy,
stay safe yourself
and don't trust to luck.
These are my views, opposed to yours—
it's an old debate.
But now,   200
why do you want to murder these children?
What have they done to you?
I grant you're smart in one way: a coward yourself,
you fear the sons of a hero.
Still,
this lies heavy on us—to die for your cowardice!
You would be the one to die,
if Zeus were just.
But let's say you're determined to take over this country—
then allow us to go into exile.   210
You should beware of violence you know,
the wind may change.
God might come round on you.
PHEU! [*cry*]
O land of Kadmos (yes I reproach you too!)
is this how you defend Herakles and his children?

Herakles who all alone fought off the Minyans
and let Thebes look through the eyes of freedom.
Nor can I praise Greece—Greece is a coward!
Greece should have come with fire and sword
to help these poor little birds of his,   220
in return for all he did—
he cleared the sea, he changed the world!
O little ones, they do not avail you,
not Thebes, not Greece.
You look to me, a weak old man,
a whisper of a man.
Strength left me some while back.
I tremble, I blur.
But if I were young,
still master of my body,   230
I'd bloody that fair head of his,
I'd run him out of town at the end of my spear!

CHORUS

Slow start, good speech.

LYKOS

Towers of words.
I will use actions.
Here! [*to Servants*] you—go to Helikon and you to Parnassos.
Tell the woodsmen there to cut logs of oak.
Bring them here, pile up wood
around the altar and set it on fire.
Burn these people alive! So they realize   240
no dead man is going to rule this land.
I am master here.
And you defiant old men

will be groaning not just for Herakles' children
but for your own house
as it falls. Remember,
you are my slaves.

CHORUS

O sons of earth, whom Ares once sowed
with teeth ripped out of the dragon's jaw,
stand up now! Break this man's ungodly head—   250
he's no Theban. A foreigner! Evil!
You will never lord it over me.
You will not enjoy the work of my hands.
Go back where you came from,
use your arrogance there.
While I'm alive, you shall not kill Herakles' children—
he isn't buried so deep.
He did good for this land.
You ravaged it, robbed him.
Am I a troublemaker if I help a friend in need?   260
O right hand, how you long to grip the spear!
But weakness kills longing.
Else I would have stopped you calling me a slave
and we'd live happily in Thebes.
But here you strut.
This city must have lost its mind
to put up with your despotism.

MEGARA

Old men, I thank you. Friends ought to show
righteous anger on their friends' behalf.
I only hope your rage does not cause you suffering.   270
But Amphitryon,

hear me. Think.
I love my children, how could I not?
And death is awful. Yet
to strive against the necessary turn of things
is simply stupid.
Yes we must die but there is no need
to die mutilated by fire—a laughingstock to our enemies!
That's worse than death.
We owe our house a finer dignity than that.   280
You have known glory in war—unbearable
for you to die as a coward.
And my husband, whose fame needs no witness,
would prefer these children not be saved
if the price is dishonor.
It breaks a good parent's heart to see children disgraced.
I must take my husband's example.
Look,
you think your son will come back from Hades?
What dead man comes back?   290
Or do you hope to soften up Lykos?
Not likely. When your enemy is a savage, flee him.
With men of culture
you can negotiate, they have a sense of shame!
It had occurred to me
we might plead for exile for the children.
But wouldn't that be worse—
to trap them in a salvation made of abject poverty?
You know the saying, people in exile
get one day of smiling from their friends.   300
Dare death with me.
Death stands by you anyway.
I call on your greatness of soul, old man.

He who battles fate shows courage,
but the courage of a fool.
No one will ever make necessity not happen.

CHORUS

Had I strength in my arms and someone were assaulting you,
I'd stop it.
But I am nothing. Now it's your task,
Amphitryon, to thrust a way through this bad luck. 310

AMPHITRYON

Not cowardice or love of life
prevents me dying: I want to save the children of my son—
impossible as this seems.
Look! You have a sword, here's my neck—
stab me! murder me! throw me from a cliff!
But grant us one favor, king, we pray.
Kill us first, before the children.
We cannot watch that.
Unholy sight—their souls
breaking free of life 320
as they call out to us.
And the rest—if you're set on it—do it.
We haven't the strength not to die.

MEGARA

I add a prayer:
you,
grant us this alone.
Let me dress my children for death.
Open the doors (we are locked out)
and allow them this much at least of their father's wealth.

LYKOS

    It shall be so. I instruct my servants to unbar the doors.   330
    Go in and dress, I do not begrudge you clothing.
    When you are ready
    I shall hand you on to the world below.

[exit Lykos by side entrance]

MEGARA

    Children, come with me
    into your father's house.
    It is still ours in name.

AMPHITRYON

    O Zeus, in vain I shared my wife with you!
    In vain I shared my son.
    Your love is not what it seemed.
    In fact I surpass you in virtue—and you a god! A big god.   340
    Herakles' children I did not betray.
    But you—you know how to sneak into other men's beds,
    how to get whatever sex you want,
    but not how to save your own kin.
    For a god, you're an idiot. Or simply immoral.

[exit Amphitryon, Megara, children into house]

CHORUS [*first choral ode*]

    Sing sorrow! on top of joy.
    So Apollo sings
    driving the gold pick into his beautiful voicing lyre.
    And I sing
    of the man who went underground, down to the dark—   350

whether I call him son of Zeus
or of Amphitryon.
I want to place a crown of praise upon his labors.
To sing of noble actions
is a glory for the dead.

First he cleared out the lion
from the grove of Zeus
and hooded himself
in its big yellow jaws.

Laid low the wild mountain centaurs   360
with arrows of blood,
arrows like wings—
those monsters known
to the long barren fields,
to the river,
to the farms,
to the grasslands
where they filled their hands with pine branches
and rode Thessaly down.

Shot the deer with golden horns   370
that used to ravage men,
and offered it to Artemis
who kills wild things.
Broke the mares of Diomedes,
bridling their bloody jaws,
their murder meals,
their man-eating joy—
their tables of evil.
Crossed the river Hebros

where the streams run silver, 380
working for his lord of Mykenai.

Slew Kyknos
on the Melian shore,
whose hospitality was
to chop his guests in bits.

Went west to the halls of evening,
where the Hesperides sing
and plucked a gold fruit
from apple branches.
Killed the snake with fiery scales 390
that coiled its coils there.
Sank through the sea
and set a calmness on the lives of sailors.

Drove his hand straight up through heaven
in Atlas' place
and held the starry houses of the gods
aloft all by himself.

Hunted the Amazon army
across rivers and rivers,
to the other side of a hostile sea, 400
gathering every Greek as he went—
hunting
the goldchased belt of the daughter of war.
Her wild gold spoil fell to him,
kept in Mykenai to this day.

Burned to death the thousand heads

of the deadly dog of Lerna.
Dipped his arrows in her poison
to kill threebodied Geryon.

Other races, other glories, he ran, he won.   410
Now's he sailed to Hades,
place of tears—
last of his labors.
He comes not back.
His house stands empty.
Charon waits.
The journey waits.
The children wait—
looking to you!
You, gone.   420

If only I had the power of youth
to shake my spear
and join my comrades,
I'd stand and save these children—force on force!
But as it is
I lack myself.

Here they come dressed for death,
once the sons of magnificent Herakles.
Here is his wife, pulling them along,
and the old father.   430
Oh sad pity.
I cannot restrain my tears,
my old man's tears.

[enter Megara, children, Amphitryon from house]

MEGARA

Well then where is our priest? Where is our sacrificer?
We stand ready to make our offerings to Hades.
Strange-looking death group.
Old men, mothers, children all together.
Grotesque fate.
I look on you for the last time.
I gave you birth, I reared you up, for enemies   440
to mock, outrage and murder.
PHEU! [cry]
All the hopes fell wrong,
the hopes we had your father and I.
He would have left you Argos when he died,
and Eurystheus' palace to rule,
with power over rich Pelasgia
and that famous lionskin that he himself
used to pull over your head.
You would be king in chariotloving Thebes,   450
possessor of all my lands,
for you were always asking him for this
and he used to play with you,
putting his big carved club into your hand.
And to you he promised Oichalia,
captured once with bow and arrows.
Three sons, three kingdoms: he had a grand design.
And I
would have chosen your brides and made you marriages
with Athens and Sparta and Thebes   460
to anchor fast your happy lives.
These things are gone.
Luck turns. Luck gave you deaths as brides,
my tears as bridal bath.

Your father's father welcomes Hades to the wedding feast—
dread father of the bride!
O little ones, which of you should I take to my heart first,
which last, or kiss, or hold?
How I wish like a bee I could gather you—
all my heartbreak for you into one teardrop.   470
O Herakles, beloved, if you hear a voice down there,
I call to you.
Your father is dying, your children are doomed, and I.
I who was once called *blessed* because of you.
Help us! Come back! Even as a shadow,
even as a dream.
They are vile men who destroy your sons.

AMPHITRYON

Make your prayers to those below, woman.
I shall spike my hand to Zeus—Zeus! if you do intend
to help us, it's almost too late!   480
But you've heard this. I waste my breath.
Death has us in its necessary grip.
Old men,
life is a small thing.
Go through it as sweetly as possible,
day into night without pain.
Time does not know how to keep our hopes safe,
but flutters off on its own business.
Look at me: I had fame, I did deeds.
Luck stripped me bare   490
as a wing to the air
in one day.
Wealth, glory—nothing is sure.
You are looking at me for the last time, old friends.

MEGARA

EA! [*scream*]
Old man! I see him! Or what am I saying!

AMPHITRYON

I don't know. I'm struck dumb.

MEGARA

Him! The one who was under the ground!
Or is it some dream in daylight—
what am I saying? What kind of dream? Am I crazy?   500
No, it is—your son, old man, no other!
Run, children, hurry, hold tight to his clothes,
don't let go!
He is no less than Zeus the Savior come to us!

[*enter Herakles from side entrance*]

HERAKLES

O house O halls O hearth of mine!
How glad I am to see you in the light!
[*cry*]
What's this. Here are my children out in front
dressed in black.
I see my wife in a crowd of men,
my father in tears—   510
what's wrong?
Woman, what is happening here?

MEGARA

O beloved!

AMPHITRYON

O light of your father!

MEGARA

You have come, you are safe, you can save us!

HERAKLES

What do you mean? Father, what is this turmoil?

MEGARA

We were lost! Old man, forgive me
if I break in.
Females are better at lament than men.
And death was on us—my children and me!   520

HERAKLES

Apollo! What a beginning!

MEGARA

My brothers are dead, my father is dead.

HERAKLES

How? What killed them?

MEGARA

Lykos. The new king here.

HERAKLES

In war? Revolution?

MEGARA

Civil war. He took power in Thebes.

HERAKLES

But why are you and my father in a terror?

MEGARA

He intended to kill us and the children.

HERAKLES

What did he fear from my sons?

MEGARA

That they one day seek to avenge Kreon. 530

HERAKLES

And why are you in funeral clothes?

MEGARA

We dressed ourselves for death.

HERAKLES

Death by violence? What horror.

MEGARA

We were all alone. We heard you were dead.

HERAKLES

You despaired of me?

MEGARA

Heralds proclaimed your death again and again.

HERAKLES

And why did you leave my house and hearth?

MEGARA

He forced us, threw your father out of bed—

HERAKLES

He had no shame, even before an old man?

MEGARA

Shame? Lykos? He stays clear of that.   540

HERAKLES

And where were my friends then?

MEGARA

Who has friends in bad times?

HERAKLES

Do they make so little of the wars I won for them?

MEGARA

I say it again, bad luck has no friends.

HERAKLES

Throw off those wreaths of death!
Look to the light! No shadows now,
it's time for me to change things!
First I'll raze this upstart tyrant's house,
cut off his unholy head
and toss it to the dogs.   550
Then all those men of Kadmos who made good off me
will fall beneath my bow of victory—
watch the arrows fly!
Until the river is thick with corpses

and the fountains run red with blood!
Who else should I defend if not wife,
sons, father? Farewell my labors!
That was all pointless.
I should have been here.
How is it heroic   560
to fight hydras and lions for Eurystheus,
while my children face death alone?
I shall never be called "Herakles the victor" again.

CHORUS

Help your family, that's the right thing.

AMPHITRYON

How like you my son, to love your friends
and hate your enemies. But don't rush in.

HERAKLES

Am I rushing in?

AMPHITRYON

Lykos has allies, desperate men,
who staged a revolution and brought this city down,
hoping to milk their fellow citizens dry.   570
Watch out!
You were seen coming in. Enemies gather.

HERAKLES

I don't care if the whole city saw me!
But I noticed a bird, a weird bird, on my way here.
Made me feel strange.
So in fact I came secretly.

AMPHITRYON

Good. Now go in and greet your hearth.
Let the house look on you.
Soon Lykos arrives with his murder plan.
Just wait: everything will unfold   580
around you.
Don't stir up the city, child,
until everything here is clear.

HERAKLES

Well advised. I'll go inside.
I am returned to life
from the sunless hole of Hades underground:
it would be disrespectful to the gods of my house
if I did not greet them.

AMPHITRYON

Did you really go into the house of Hades?

HERAKLES

Yes, and brought back the threeheaded dog.   590

AMPHITRYON

Did you do battle, or was it a gift?

HERAKLES

I did battle. And won because I had seen the mysteries.

AMPHITRYON

Where is the dog now—at Eurystheus' house?

HERAKLES

No, in the sacred grove of Hermione.

AMPHITRYON

And Eurystheus knows you've returned to the world?

HERAKLES

No he does not. I came here first.

AMPHITRYON

Why were you so long underground?

HERAKLES

I had to bring Theseus back with me from Hades.

AMPHITRYON

Is he gone home?

HERAKLES

Gone gladly home, to Athens.   600
But come, children, let us go in. Into your father's house.
How beautiful are entrances,
compared to exits!
Be strong, don't cry.
And you, dear wife, gather yourself,
no more trembling, let go my clothes.
I have no wings, I shall not fly away.
Ah,
but they do not let go, they hold tight to my clothes.
Did you come so close to the razor's edge?   610
Here, I will take your hands and lead you
like a big ship towing little boats behind.

Herakles

You are my care, I do not deny it.
All men are equal in this—good or bad
they love their children.
Money brings difference—some have it, some don't.
But humankind is one in loving children.

[exit Herakles with children, Megara, Amphitryon into house]

CHORUS (*second choral ode*)
                    I loved being young.
            Old age weighs like the rock of Aetna
                    on my head, on my eyes   620
                    a shadowy cloak.
            I would not take a tyrant's opulence
                    or houses filled with gold
                    in place of youth.
            Beautiful to be young in wealth,
            beautiful to be young in poverty.
                    Old age I hate—
                disgusting deathbound age—
    let it slide under the waves, vanish from houses and cities,
            spin off into the air and be gone!   630

            If the gods knew what men know,
                    they'd grant a second youth
                    to a life of virtue.
        So a good man would die then come back—run
    a second race—while the ignoble go once around the track
                    and stop.
            By this you could distinguish worthless men
                from good—as sailors know the stars
            that sail through broken clouds at night.

But as things are, the gods set no clear line   640
between good men and bad.
Life goes rolling on,
exalting only money.

I shall not stop
mingling the Muses with the Graces—
sweetest of connections.
I could not live without music,
I could not be without crowns of praise.
Yes I am old
but I'll sing forth Memory,   650
sing forth Herakles' beautiful victory
with wine and lyres and flutes and song—
I will not stop singing
the Muses who set me dancing.

Paeans for Apollo
the women of Delos sing
at his temple gates
as they wheel round in the beautiful dances.
Paeans for your house
shall I sing   660
as an old swan lifts its white throat.
Excellence rises up into hymns of praise:
he is son of Zeus!
But far beyond his birth he labored for mortals
and gave us lives of peacefulness,
clear of beasts and terror.

[enter Lykos from side entrance, enter Amphitryon from house]

LYKOS

Just in time, Amphitryon.
You've been a long while inside
decking yourselves for death.
Go call out Herakles' wife and sons.   670
That was our agreement.

AMPHITRYON

King, you persecute in me a poor sad man
and you insult the dead.
Yes you are in power here but temper yourself.
Our death is your decree,
we acquiesce. It must be as you say.

LYKOS

Where is Megara? Where are the children?

AMPHITRYON

I would guess—

LYKOS

Guess what?

AMPHITRYON

—she's at the hearth making supplication—   680

LYKOS

Useless if she begs for life.

AMPHITRYON

—and calling on her dead husband. No point in that either.

LYKOS

No, he won't show up.

AMPHITRYON

Unless some god resurrects him.

LYKOS

Go in and bring her out.

AMPHITRYON

That would make me an accomplice in her death.

LYKOS

All right, if you're so sensitive,
I'll go.
Servants, follow.
Let's get this over with.   690

[exit Lykos into house]

AMPHITRYON

You go, that's right.
Someone will see to you!
The evil you are is the evil you get.
Old men, this is perfect:
Lykos caught in a net made of swords,
the despicable coward!
I shall go and watch his body fall.
Sweet to see an enemy pay the price.

[exit Amphitryon into house]

Herakles

CHORUS (*third choral ode*)
Reversal of evils! The once great tyrant
    turns his life toward death!   700
        O!
            Justice flows back!
              Doom sent by gods!
                You and your arrogance
            arrive at the place of just reprisal.
        Joy pours from my eyes.
    Herakles lives! I had no hope.
    But he came up from hell!
Old men, we should go look inside.

LYKOS
    IO MOI MOI! [*cry from inside*]   710

CHORUS
    I love to hear this sound beginning in the house.
        Death is close.
            He cries out.
              Murder now.

LYKOS
    [*from inside*] Land of Kadmos, I am caught! I die!

CHORUS
           Yes you die. As you would have killed.
              You are paying the price of your own deeds.
           Enjoy it!
         Who says the gods are not strong?
        Old men, the unholy tyrant is no more.   720

Silence in the house. Let us turn to dancing.
Our loved ones prosper!

Dances, dances, feasts and dances
   fill the holy town of Thebes!
      Change of tears,
         change of luck,
            brings forth songs.
         Gone is the upstart, our king rules again!
      For he escaped the lake of death—
   outside all imagining   730
hope is here!

Gods, gods are giving heed
   to what is unjust, to what is holy.
      Gold and the good life
         drag men out of their right minds—
            the lure of power!
         None dares to think how time may flip him over—
      racing past the law
   he smashes
the black car of his luck.   740

O river Ismenos come with your crowns!
   Dance, you polished streets of Thebes!
      Dance, river Dirke with your lovely streams!
         Come daughters of the rivers of Asopos—
            sing with me
               the beautiful agony
                  of Herakles the victor!
                     O rock of Pytho,

home of the Muses,
exalt my city with a shout of joy, 750
where dragon's teeth sprang up
as men of war
and bequeathed this land
to the children of their children—
a holy light for Thebes.

O bridal bed shared by two bridegrooms—
a mortal and Zeus,
who both came into the nymph Alkmene.
How true, O Zeus, this marriage proves to be!
I had no hope 760
but now I see!
Bright power of Herakles!
You came up from hell,
you left death's house,
you showed yourself a better king
than that ignoble man.
And this will be clear
in the contest of swords—
if justice
is still pleasing to the gods. 770

[enter Iris and Madness above the house]

CHORUS
EA EA! [*cry*]
Look!
Terror!
What kind of apparition is that above the house?

Run! Run! Lift your feet!
Lord Apollo protect me!

IRIS

Calm down, old men.
This is Madness, daughter of Night.
I am Iris, servant of the gods.
We do not come to harm your city.   780
Against one man we have a war to wage—
the so-called son of Zeus and Alkmene.
Until he finished with his bitter labors,
his destiny protected Herakles
and Zeus did not let me or Hera harm him.
But now he is done with the tasks of Eurystheus,
Hera wants to stain him in the blood
of his own children.
So do I.
Come then,   790
unmarriageable daughter of black Night,
make your heart hard.
Drive insanity into this man—throw
childkilling chaos into his mind and his jumping feet!
Pay out the rope of blood
by which he'll pull his children into Hades
with his own hand.
So he may come to know the rage of Hera,
my rage too!
Either gods are nothing and mortals prevail,   800
or this man has to pay a price.

MADNESS

I come from good parents: my mother is Night

and my father is Heaven.
But my functions make me generally repulsive.
And I do not enjoy the visits I pay to poor human beings.
Yet please, hear me, before you and Hera
make a mistake.
This man is famous, on earth and among the gods.
You are launching me against a man
who civilized the trackless earth and savage sea,   810
who lifted up all by himself the honors of the gods
when impious people let them fall.
Renounce these evil plans.

IRIS

Hera and I don't need your advice.

MADNESS

I want to set you both on a better path.

IRIS

Hera didn't send you here to practice sanity.

MADNESS

As the sun is my witness, I act against my will.
But if I must serve you and Hera,
I go.
Wilder than the wild cracking sea,   820
than earth split open,
than the lightning bolt that breathes pain,
is the race I shall run into the breast of Herakles!
I'll smash his halls, pull down the house,
kill the children.

And the killer will not know who it is he kills
until my madness ends.
Watch!
he tosses his head! he's at the starting post!—
eyes rolling back.   830
breath heaving up, like a bull at the charge—
he bellows!
I call upon the dooms of death
to howl in like dogs to the hunt.
Soon I will set you dancing, my man, yes
I will turn you into a flute of fear!
Off with you to Olympos, Iris.
As into Herakles' house
unseen
I sink.   840

[exit Iris and Madness]

CHORUS
OTOTOTOI! [cry]
He is cut down!
Your flower, your son of Zeus,
O Greece, you are losing your one true hero—
he dances to the flutes of madness now!

She's off!
The chariot moves,
the lash falls,
she's driving toward ruin
like a gorgon of Night!   850
Hissing of a hundred snakes around her head!

Eyes that will turn you to stone!
In an instant, luck changes.
In an instant, children die.

AMPHITRYON
IO MOI MELEOS! [*from within, a cry*]

CHORUS
O Zeus! Your child is childless now.
Insane rawflesh-eating unjust revenge
is going to lay him out.

AMPHITRYON
IO! [*cry*] O halls!

CHORUS
Now it begins—the dance with no drums,   860
no delight!

AMPHITRYON
IO! [*cry*] O house!

CHORUS
To the blood she goes—
no wine of Dionysos here!

AMPHITRYON
Run, children, out of the way!

CHORUS
Here they are the flutes of ruin!

He is hunting his children down.
Madness runs her Bacchic revel to its end
in this house.

AMPHITRYON
AIAI KAKON! [*cry*] O evils!   870

CHORUS
AIAI! [*cry*]
How I grieve for the old man,
for the mother who bore these children
pointlessly.
Look, look—
a storm shakes the house, the roof falls!

AMPHITRYON
E E! [*scream*]
What are you doing here, child of Zeus, Pallas Athena,
sending upon this house
a chaos of hell!   880

[enter Messenger from the house]

MESSENGER
Old men—

CHORUS
Why do you call?

MESSENGER
Abominations in the house!

CHORUS

You tell my fears.

MESSENGER

The children are dead.

CHORUS

AIAI! [*scream*]

MESSENGER

Grieve, yes.

CHORUS

Foul murders!
Foul father's hands.

MESSENGER

No words can say.   890

CHORUS

But please tell me somehow,
this ruin—
tell me how did it rush from God
upon the house and these poor children?

MESSENGER

Sacrifices had been set before the altar of Zeus
to purify the house, because Herakles murdered
Lykos inside.
There stood the children as beautiful as a chorus,
and the old man and Megara. The altar basket
had gone round. They kept holy silence.   900

He stood perfectly still,
about to dip the torch in the water.
Everyone stared.
And all of a sudden he changed.
His eye rolled back to the blood roots.
Foam dripped from his chin.
And he spoke with a manic laugh:
"Father, why should I sacrifice before killing Eurystheus?
Why double the work of cleansing the house?
I can finish all this at a single blow.   910
I'll bring the head of Eurystheus here,
add it to this corpse, then purify my hands.
Empty that water. Drop the baskets.
Who'll give me my bow? Where are my weapons?
I'm going to Mykenai! I need crowbars,
pickaxes—that Kyklopean masonry is solid!
But I'll smash it down with my irons!"
Then in his mind he saw a chariot,
mounted it, rode off,
lashing with an imaginary whip.   920
The servants were caught between laughter and panic—
glancing at one another—
"Is the master playing or has he gone mad?"
Up and down the rooms he ranged
and thought he had come to the city of Nisos,
though he was in fact in the midst of his own house.
He lay on the floor and imagined he was feasting.
This went on awhile, then he claimed he was
approaching the Isthmos.
There he stripped himself naked   930
and engaged in a wrestling match with no one,
proclaiming himself victor over no one,

bowing to an audience of no one.
Then roaring out curses at Eurystheus
he declared he'd come to Mykenai.
His father touched his hand and said,
"O child what's happening to you? What is this strangeness?
Has the blood of your killings made you mad?"
But taking him for the father of Eurystheus
Herakles thrust him off   940
and got out his bow to use against the children—
thought they were Eurystheus' children—
darting in terror this way and that,
one to his mother's robes, one to the shade of a pillar,
one hunched under the altar like a little bird.
The mother screamed, "You are their father!
Do you kill your own sons?"
Then the old man screamed. The servants screamed.
But he circled the pillar to get at his son
and with a dreadful pivoting move   950
shot him right through the liver.
The child fell back
and stained the stones red.
Herakles let out a war cry:
"That's the first one dead of Eurystheus' litter—
to repay me for his father's abuse!"
Then he aimed his bow at another child
crouching by the altar as if he could hide.
This one ran out and reached for his father's
knee, chin, neck, wailing,   960
"Don't kill me father—
I'm yours, not Eurystheus' son!"
But he, with a blank gorgon stare,
took his club (the boy stood too close for the bow)

and like a blacksmith at his forge
brought it down on the small fair head,
smashing the bones.
Now the second son was dead,
he went for the third.
But the poor mother grabbed her child   970
into the house and shut the doors.
Then he, as if assaulting the Kyklopean walls themselves,
levered up the doorframes and tore out the posts
and laid mother and child low with a single arrow.
And at that point he was ready to ride down his father
but there came a phantasm—it looked like Athena—
shaking a spear above her helmet
she hurled a rock. It hit Herakles' chest,
stopped his death rage.
Knocked him out.   980
He fell and
hit a pillar that lay snapped in two.
And we, now freed from running for our lives,
lashed him to the pillar with the old man's help.
So when he wakes from sleep he won't do any more.
He sleeps. Sleeps!—
what sleep is that!
I do not know a man alive more cursed.

[exit Messenger by side entrance]

CHORUS (*fourth choral ode*)
There was a murder done in Argos once
by the daughters of Danaos—   990
everyone has heard of it, incredible yes.
But these evils here

belonging to the son of Zeus
go far beyond
anything in the past.

I could tell of the murder of Prokne's only son
as sacrifice to the Muses.
But you, O man of death,
took your three sons together
in the mad work.   1000
AIAI! [*cry*]
What groaning,
what lament,
what song of death,
what dance of Hades
shall I do?

[doors of house open, revealing Herakles amid bodies]

CHORUS
PHEU PHEU! [*cry*]
Look, the doors slide open.
[*cry*]
Look, the poor children lie
before their father.   1010
Look at him sleeping his dread sleep.
Knots, cords, cables
lash the Heraklean body to the pillars of his house.
IO MOI! [*cry*]
And here comes the old man like a bitter late bird
lamenting its
unfledged young.

[enter Amphitryon from house]

AMPHITRYON

Silence, silence, old men of Kadmos.
Will you not leave him sleep.

CHORUS

I weep for you   1020
and for the children
and for the beautiful victor himself.

AMPHITRYON

Back off, don't make noise,
don't cry out.
He sleeps.
Do not wake him.

CHORUS

OIMOI! [*cry*]
So much blood.

AMPHITRYON

A A! [*cry*]
You destroy me.   1030

CHORUS

Blood poured out, blood rising up.

AMPHITRYON

Quietly, old men.
If he wakes and breaks his bonds he will destroy the city,
destroy his father, pull the roof beams down.

CHORUS

This is all impossible.

AMPHITRYON

Silence, I want to listen to his breathing.

CHORUS

Is he asleep?

AMPHITRYON

A death sleep, a murder sleep,
the sleep of the slaughtering bow.

CHORUS

Groan now. 1040

AMPHITRYON

Yes.

CHORUS

For the death of children—

AMPHITRYON

OMOI! [*cry*]

CHORUS

and for your son.

AMPHITRYON

AIAI! [*cry*]

CHORUS
   O old man—

AMPHITRYON
   Silence, silence.
   He is moving, he wakes! Quick,
   I shall hide!

CHORUS
   Courage.   1050
   Night still presses on his eyes.

AMPHITRYON
   Careful, careful—it's not death I fear
   on this day of evils.
   But if he murders his own father
   what bloodguilt is added to the pain he has now!
   What vengeance!

CHORUS
   You should have died the day you sacked
   the city of the Taphians.

AMPHITRYON
   Run old men, get out of the way!
   The mad man wakes!   1060
   Soon he'll be throwing murder on murder,
   he'll set the city of Kadmos dancing a mad Bacchic dance!

HERAKLES
   EA! [*strange sound*]

I can breathe. I can see.
Here is air. Ground. Rays of sun.
But I feel like I've fallen down a deep wave
into a big choppy sea.
My breath is hot,
it shakes my lungs.
Look—why do I sit like a ship at its moorings,   1070
lashed to a piece of half-smashed stone?
Why are these corpses here?—
and my bow and arrows littered on the ground,
trusty old friends.
Surely I haven't gone back to Hades—
done a second lap on Eurystheus' racecourse?
No, I don't see any rock of Sisyphos.
No Pluto. No Persephone.
I'm lost. Where in the world is Herakles ever lost?
Someone! Help me!   1080
It's all gone strange.

AMPHITRYON
  Old men, should I go near?

CHORUS
  Yes, I'll go with you.

HERAKLES
  Father, why do you wipe your eyes?
  Why do you stand so far off?

AMPHITRYON
  O child. You are mine, though you do evil.

HERAKLES

What do I do that makes your tears run down?

AMPHITRYON

Even a god would groan if he knew.

HERAKLES

It sounds terrible, yet you do not say.

AMPHITRYON

You yourself can see, if your mind is clear now.   1090

HERAKLES

You're hinting at some new condition of life?

AMPHITRYON

If you're no longer drunk with death, I can speak.

HERAKLES

Papa, stop riddling!

AMPHITRYON

I'm not sure of your mind.

HERAKLES

My mind? I don't recall losing my mind.

AMPHITRYON

Old men, should I undo the ropes?

HERAKLES

And tell me who tied them—this is an insult!

AMPHITRYON

You have trouble enough, let that go.

HERAKLES

But will you tell me what's going on?

AMPHITRYON

O Zeus on your throne, do you see these deeds done by
Hera?   1100

HERAKLES

Hostility from *her*?

AMPHITRYON

Never mind Hera. Hera is not the point now.

HERAKLES

What are you leading up to?

AMPHITRYON

Look now, look at these children's bodies.

HERAKLES

OIMOI! [*cry*]
What is this I see?

AMPHITRYON

You have waged war on your own sons, my child.

HERAKLES

What war do you mean? Who killed them?

AMPHITRYON

You and your bow and one of the gods.

HERAKLES

What are you saying? What have I done? Father!   1110

AMPHITRYON

You went mad.

HERAKLES

And killed my wife too?

AMPHITRYON

All this is the work of one hand.

HERAKLES

AIAI! [*cry*]
My world goes dark.

AMPHITRYON

I groan for you.

HERAKLES

Did I wreck the house in madness?

AMPHITRYON

I know one thing: all is grief for you.

HERAKLES

Where did the frenzy seize me?

AMPHITRYON

    By the altar, you were purifying your hands.   1120

HERAKLES

    OIMOI! [*cry*]

    Why spare my life?

    I've become the murderer of my own beloveds.

    Shall I not be their avenger too?

    Let me throw myself off a cliff

    or drive a sword through my liver

    or burn the scandal out of my flesh with fire!

    But here

    comes someone.

    Obstacle   1130

    to my plans for death.

    It's Theseus, kinsman and friend—

    I'll be seen!

    I'll pollute his eyes!

    OIMOI! [*cry*]

    Can I take wing, or disappear underground?

    Here, I'll pull a shadow over my head.

    Shame oh shame.

    I do not want to throw bloodguilt

    on an innocent man.   1140

[enter Theseus from side entrance]

THESEUS

    I came here with others—left them by the Asopos river,

    young warriors of Athens

    to support your son, old man, with spears.

    For a rumor reached our city

that Lykos had stolen the scepter of this land
and made war on you.
I owe a debt of gratitude to Herakles:
he brought me up alive from underground—
so in case he has need
of my hand or my allies,   1150
I've come.
EA! [*cry*]
Why is the ground covered in corpses?
Have I come too late?
Who killed these children?
Whose woman was this?

AMPHITRYON

O king of the hill of olives—

THESEUS

You sound so solemn.

AMPHITRYON

We have suffered. Sorrowful things. From the gods.

THESEUS

Whose children are these?   1160

AMPHITRYON

My poor son begot them.
Begot them and murdered them in their blood.

THESEUS

What are you saying? What did he do?

AMPHITRYON

Went stark mad.
Used the poisoned arrows.

THESEUS

Dreadful words.

AMPHITRYON

We are finished, vanished, gone.

THESEUS

Hush.

AMPHITRYON

Yes, hush.

THESEUS

This agony comes from Hera.   1170
Who is that lying there?

AMPHITRYON

My poor, my poor beleaguered son.
Who fought beside the gods at Phlegraia
where giants died.

THESEUS

PHEU PHEU! [*cry*]
What man more cursed than this!

AMPHITRYON

You could not find another human being
so struck down, so lost.

THESEUS

    Why does he hide his head in his robe?

AMPHITRYON

    Shame before your eyes.   1180
    Shame before your kinship.
    Shame for the blood of his sons.

THESEUS

    But if I came to share his grief?
    Uncover him.

AMPHITRYON

    O child, take the robe from your eyes,
    let it fall, show your face to the sun.
    Here is a counterweight to tears.
    I supplicate your chin, your knee, your hand,
    and I weep as an old man weeps.
    My child,   1190
    press down that lion heart.
    It races you on to blood and death,
    linking evil with evil. O my son.

THESEUS

    You crouch in misery, I call you—
    show your face to a friend.
    There is no cloud so black
    it could hide your misfortune.
    Why do you wave me off?
    You fear to pollute me?
    I don't care about that. I'll share your bad luck—   1200
    I shared your good luck once,

when you brought me from the dead world back to life.
Hateful to me is a gratitude that grows old.
A friend who enjoys your prosperity
but refuses to sail with your grief.
Stand up. Uncover your poor head.
Look at me. This is nobility in a man:
to bear what falls from the gods and not say No.

HERAKLES
Theseus, have you seen this agony of my children?

THESEUS
I have seen and heard.   1210

HERAKLES
Then why uncover my head to the sun?

THESEUS
Why? Because as a mortal you cannot pollute the gods.

HERAKLES
Reckless man, flee my unholy pollution.

THESEUS
There is no spirit of vengeance that goes from friend to friend.

HERAKLES
Theseus, I thank you.
How right I was to help you once.

THESEUS
I was lucky then, I pity you now.

HERAKLES

You pity me although I killed my children?

THESEUS

I weep for your whole changed life.

HERAKLES

Have you seen a man more ruined?   1220

THESEUS

Your misfortunes could touch the sky.

HERAKLES

That's why it is time for me to end things.

THESEUS

Threats are no use, the gods don't care.

HERAKLES

Gods are stubborn. So am I.

THESEUS

Quiet, lest you get more suffering.

HERAKLES

I am stuffed with evils—nowhere to put more.

THESEUS

What will you do? Where will your passion take you?

HERAKLES

To death, whence I came, under the ground.

THESEUS

Your words are banal.

HERAKLES

Don't lecture me, safe from sadness as you are.   1230

THESEUS

Is this the all-heroic Herakles talking?

HERAKLES

Not *all*-heroic. There has to be some limit to pain.

THESEUS

Is this the great benefactor of mankind?

HERAKLES

What good is mankind? It is Hera who rules.

THESEUS

Greece would not allow you to die so stupid a death.

HERAKLES

Listen, here is my answer.
Here is my life—*not worth living*
now or ever.
First, I came into being from this sort of man:
he killed my mother's father   1240
then married her to deflect the guilt.
When the family foundations are so poor
of course the descendants turn out a disaster.
And Zeus—whoever Zeus is!—begot me
(don't be offended, old man, I consider you

my father now, not Zeus)
as an enemy for Hera.
While I was still an infant
she put snakes into my cradle, that wife of Zeus,
to annihilate me.   1250
And when I grew up—all those labors,
what can I say? Those lions.
Those typhons.
Those giants.
Those centaurs.
Those wars.
Then the hydra with her hundred heads snapping.
And down to hell to get the threeheaded dog.
And now, absolutely last labor.
I kill my children.   1260
I finish my house in evil.

This is where I've come to in necessity.

It is unholy for me to keep living in Thebes, my beloved Thebes.
What temple, what assembly, could I enter?
I am unapproachably cursed.
Then should I go to Argos? How, since I'm banished?
So set out for some other city
where I'll be recognized, despised,
assaulted by bitter tongues?
"Isn't that the son of Zeus, the one who killed his children   1270
and his wife? Ruin take him!"
I can see my life coming to this:
the ground itself will cry out in a voice
forbidding me to touch it,

the seas and rivers will deny me crossing!
I shall be like Ixion,
bound on a wheel.
Why stay alive? What good is there
in a life both useless and unholy?
Let the brilliant wife of Zeus dance   1280
and pound Olympos with her feet!
She got what she wanted—
smashed the greatest man in Greece
and turned his life upside down.
Who could pray to her?
For the sake of another woman,
for the sake of sex and jealousy,
she has annihilated the best friend Greece ever had.
And he was innocent.

CHORUS

   This strife came from no one but Hera—he's right.   1290

THESEUS

   My advice is, endure it.
   No mortal is untouched by changes of luck,
   no god either—if poets tell the truth.
   Don't gods sleep in one another's beds?
   Don't they throw their fathers into chains
   and take their power? But all the same
   they occupy Olympos, they hold on,
   criminals or not.
   Will you protest your fate,
   when gods do not?   1300
   Leave Thebes then.
   Follow me to Athens.

There I shall purify your hands of blood
and give you a home and a share of my wealth—
all those treasures I got from killing the Minotaur—
and the lands apportioned to me
will be yours while you live.
And when you die, when you go down to Hades,
the whole city of Athens will exalt you
in monuments and sacrifice.   1310
We win a fair crown of glory if we help a good man.
And by this grace I repay you for saving me.
Right now you need a friend.

HERAKLES
Details!
This is all incidental to my grief.
I don't believe gods commit adultery.
I don't believe gods throw gods in chains
or tyrannize one another.
Never did believe it, never shall.
God must, if God is truly God,   1320
lack nothing.
All the rest is miserable poets' lies.
But it gives me pause,
even in this extremity,
to think dying might make me look like a coward.
Anyone who flinches from bad luck
could not stand against the weapon of an enemy.

I will go on with life.

I'll go to your city, give thanks for your grace and your gifts.
Countless were the labors I tasted.   1330

Herakles

I never said no, I never wept.
And did not think that I would come to this,
pouring down tears.
Well, it seems I am the slave of luck.
Old man, you see me exiled,
you see me murderer of my own children.
Give them burial and give them tears
(I am forbidden).
Lay them in their mother's arms.
Wretched embrace. My doing.   1340
When you have buried them,
live on in this city
however sad it is.
O children,
the father who begot you has destroyed you.
Forfeit all the goods I won for you, labor of a lifetime,
and the glorious reputation, a father's best bequest.
And you, poor woman, slaughtered:
unfair return for your service to my bed,
your long watching of my house.
OIMOI! [*cry*] for my wife and children!
OIMOI! [*cry*] for me!
Unyoked from all of you now.
O bitter last kiss.
O bitter weapons. My partners.
Should I take you with me or leave you behind?
Knocking against my ribs you will always be saying,
"This is how you slew your wife and sons,
we are your childkillers."
Can I bear that?   1360
Can I answer?
But without them

won't I die in shame at my enemies' hands—
naked, nobody?
I cannot leave them.
However grotesque it is,
I must keep my weapons.
Help me, Theseus, in one thing more—
I have to bring the monster dog to Argos.
Who knows what will happen if I'm alone with my grief.   1370
O land of Kadmos, O people of Thebes,
mourn, mourn, go to the grave of my children.
Mourn us all in one.
We are all dead.
Poor souls, hit by Hera.

THESEUS

Rise up, dear sad friend. Enough tears.

HERAKLES

I cannot. My legs won't move.

THESEUS

Luck can break even the strongest man.

HERAKLES

PHEU! [*cry*]
I wish I were stone! No memory!   1380

THESEUS

Stop. Give me your hand. I am your friend.

HERAKLES

I fear to stain your clothes with blood.

THESEUS

Stain them, I don't care.

HERAKLES

My children are gone. You are my child.

THESEUS

Put your hand on my neck, I shall lead you.

HERAKLES

Yoke of love. Though one of us is cursed.
Father, to find such a friend!

AMPHITRYON

Blessed be the place that gave him birth.

HERAKLES

Theseus, turn me, let me see the children.

THESEUS

Why? Will it heal you?   1390

HERAKLES

I long to do it. And to embrace my father.

AMPHITRYON

Yes I long for this.

THESEUS

Do you entirely forget your labors?

HERAKLES

    All my labors were less than this.

THESEUS

    You want to look like a woman?

HERAKLES

    You want me broken?

THESEUS

    The glorious Herakles is no more!

HERAKLES

    Glorious? How glorious were *you* when we were down in hell?

THESEUS

    I was the least of men.

HERAKLES

    And yet you say I am made small by grief?   1400

THESEUS

    Go.

HERAKLES

    Farewell, old man.

AMPHITRYON

    And you, my son.

HERAKLES

    Bury the children, as I said.

AMPHITRYON
Who'll bury me?

HERAKLES
I will.

AMPHITRYON
When?

HERAKLES
When you die.

AMPHITRYON
How?

HERAKLES
I'll bring you to Athens.   1410
But take these children out, poor unbearable burden.

So I, a man utterly wrecked and utterly shamed,
shall follow Theseus
like a little boat being towed along.
Whoever values wealth or strength
more than friends
is mad.

CHORUS
We go in pity, we go in tears.
For we have lost our greatest friend.

[exeunt omnes]

HEKABE

PREFACE

Vladimir: Well? Shall we go?
Estragon: Yes let's go.
[They do not move].[1]

I have had for some years on my computer a file called "Unpleas-
antness of Euripides," in which I place at random thoughts on
this subject, in hopes that the file will someday add up to an an-
swer to the question, Why is Euripides so unpleasant? Certainly
he is. Certainly I am not the only person who thinks so. Not the
only person whose heart sinks at the prospect of reading, teach-
ing or attending one of his plays. It's the same response I have to
Beckett—that sinking feeling of *oh no here we go again* as the
bleakness closes in. Aristotle may have been registering some such
impression when he mysteriously labeled Euripides *tragikotatos*,
"the most tragic" of the Greek poets. Who knows what Aristotle
meant by *tragikotatos*—experts disagree—but here's what Beckett
might have meant if he had said it:

> Tragedy is not concerned with human justice. Tragedy is
> the statement of an expiation, but not the miserable expi-
> ation of a codified breach of a local arrangement organised
> by the knaves for the fools. The tragic figure represents the
> expiation of original sin, of the original and eternal sin
> of...having been born.[2]

1. Samuel Beckett, *Waiting for Godot*, translated by Samuel Beckett (Grove, 1954), p. 59.
2. Samuel Beckett, *Proust* (London: Chatto and Windus, 1931; Calder and Boyars, 1965), p. 67.

I cite this remark because it seems to me a cogent introduction to the Euripidean Hekabe, a character who, until the final scene of this play, has committed no other sin than that of having been born. She was born to be queen of Troy at the time of the Trojan War and mother of (legendarily) fifty children, of whom she watched forty-nine flow straight down into Hades, like the character Beckett describes as "giving birth astride the grave." Her story is a war story and Euripides develops it around two of the ugliest principles that govern war stories—necessity and revenge. Necessity takes the form of a demand by the Greek warrior Achilles—who is by this time dead so the demand issues from his ghost—that a female human being should be slaughtered on his tomb as a sacrifice to himself. Revenge is embodied in Hekabe, the ancient queen of Troy whom we see transformed by the atrocities of war into a vengeance maniac. She is onstage throughout the play. At first she acts ancient, broken, hysterical. She watches her daughter Polyxena led away to be sacrificed to Achilles and falls flat on the ground in despair. Then something changes. News comes to her of the treacherous murder of her son Polydoros—the only son she had left—and suddenly she rises up, assembles herself one last time to action. She is jubilant, she is vicious, she is a shocking thing to see. Euripides pushes her to the very limit of human being and then, on the last page of the play, pushes her beyond. In the final scene Hekabe receives a prophecy that at her death she will suffer metamorphosis into a dog. She appears not to care very much about this prophecy. Her suffering for the original sin of having been born is already off the human scale. Really there is nowhere for her to go but out of the species.

Euripides' unpleasantness is a matter of technique as well as topic. He has a gift for withholding or spoiling elements of the play that we as audience want to be there or to be perfect, so that we can derive an appropriate tragic pleasure. Three such elements are: 1) a basic organization of the action 2) a recognizable hero or heroine 3) a clear moral issue.

Taking these in order. 1) Organization: Aristotle suggests a good way to organize a play is with beginning, middle, end. The *Hekabe* is a play that begins at the end. Begins at the fall of Troy. What bigger ending could there be? The world and its world war are over. Most of the Trojans are dead. Most of the Greeks have already achieved the exploits that will mark them as memorable. The characters and crises of the *Hekabe* are little more than a few leftover trickles from the carcass of a smashed civilization. Beginning at the end, this play unravels itself backwards to a condition so devoid of moral, emotional or aesthetic content, it is like a state of *pre*creation.

2) Recognizable hero or heroine: A hero/heroine is generally recognizable as the character who is onstage most (that would be Hekabe) and the character who elicits our pity and fear (that might be Hekabe or it might not; you will find her difficult to empathize with in the end). The question is confused by the presence of Polyxena, Hekabe's daughter, an absolute innocent who goes to her death in the middle of the play framed in 100 percent heroic sentiments and clearly intended to provoke our tears. Sacrificing virgins is an old trick in Greek tragedy, made use of by all three tragedians. But Euripides aims at a different effect than does Aischylos in *Agamemnon* (where Iphigeneia is slaughtered by her father) or Sophokles in *Antigone* (where Antigone is buried alive by Kreon). Iphigeneia and Antigone are sensationally significant victims: Iphigeneia's sacrifice is the lynchpin of all that happens to Agamemnon afterwards; Antigone's death is the transcendent culmination of Sophokles' play. These deaths change the stories in which they are set, transform the lives around them and force

moral reasoning to an extreme confrontation with itself. Poly-xena's death is different. It is not placed at the beginning or at the end of the play but muffled in the middle; it does not constitute either cause or culmination of the action; it does not change the plot or other people in any substantial way; and it forces us to no moral conclusion at all except that such sacrifice is irrelevant to the world in which it is staged. Polyxena is a shooting star that wipes itself across the play and disappears. And Euripides wants us to notice this—this irrelevance of Polyxena.

You can tell that he does by the fact that he has Agamemnon drop a casual remark (at line 871/903* of *Hekabe* and so hundreds of lines after Polyxena has come and gone) about the fact that the Greeks cannot presently sail home *because the winds are refusing to blow.* No fifth-century Greek could sit in the audience and hear that line and not be reminded of the other occasion on which the winds refused to blow for Agamemnon—the story made famous by Aischylos of how Agamemnon came to sacrifice Iphigeneia at the beginning of the Trojan War. Euripides wants us to mark the difference between that Agamemnon and this Aga-memnon, between the beginning and end of a war, between a tragedy by Aischylos and a tragedy by Euripides.

Aischylos lived a generation before Euripides, producing his plays in the first half of the fifth century BC—a time when the Athenians had just defeated their archenemy, the empire of Persia, and were launching themselves on several heady decades of imperial conquest, making the world safe for democracy and all that. Euripides lived in the latter half of the fifth century—in the midst of the seemingly endless Peloponnesian War between Athens and Sparta, which would outlast Euripides' lifetime, ex-terminate a generation of his fellow Greeks and bring about the

*Please note that the first set of figures given refers to the line numbers of the present translation, the second to those of the Greek text.

collapse of the empire of Athens, not to say the cultural moment that we call "classical Greece."

Aischylos looked at the story of Agamemnon and saw a parable of human grandiosity and tragic *katharsis*, leading through bloodshed and strife to an eventual restoration of civilized order. Euripides looked at the same story and saw smeared makeup. There is nothing tragic, grandiose, or even very interesting about the Agamemnon of *Hekabe*. Euripides gives us a sampling of Agamemnon's story to remind us of how much is lost from the tonal surface of this myth. Now that the big war is over, dramatic focus shifts from the victors to the victims of it, but these victims are people expelled from life and time. Their past is canceled, their future empty. They have no gods at all. They seem caught in an inertia where significant action, should it occur, has to be motivated by ghosts. There is nowhere in these characters to dig for a profound reversal or a revelatory recognition. The only tragic *katharsis* Euripides can imagine for Hekabe is to cleanse her of her very human skin—by turning her into a dog. And it seems to me that the eroded surface of this play is a comment not just on Hekabe and her sad fate, not just on the values of war at the end of a civilization, but on what Euripides thinks he's doing when he writes a play. Again he reminds me of Beckett, a playwright who felt he was living after the end of his own art form, indeed after the end of language, and who has this to say about the predicament:

> It is becoming more difficult, even senseless, for me to write a standard English. More and more my own language seems to me as a veil, to be torn apart to approach the things (or the nothings) behind it. . . . A time, let's hope, is coming when language will be best used when best abused. Since we can't eliminate it all at once, let's not neglect anything that might contribute to its corruption. To bore hole after hole

in it, until what cowers behind it begins to seep through—
I can imagine no higher goal for a contemporary writer.[3]

Hekabe's language has something of this rotted-away quality. Victors and victims carve at one another in a sort of exhausted endgame bereft of fine phrasing. Verbs are savage. Adjectives minimal. Figures rare. When Euripides does allow himself to unfold a metaphor, he does so in such a way as to decline it to bare fact. For example, in the third choral ode, he introduces the oldest metaphor in the Greek tradition for the ruin of a civilization: rape.

In Greek poetry cities were figured as female and the same word was used to denote the battlements or towers of a city and the headdress, veil or bindings that cover a woman's head. These bindings were not optional for women: to keep the head properly covered in public was a mark of civic status and sexual respectability. Within this social code, within this ancient metaphor, the integrity of women, cities and civilization is all bound up together. To rape a city is to pull off its headbinding, to wreck its crown of towers. Such a city will be as polluted as a fallen woman. Its honor is over. But of course rape is not just a metaphor in wartime. Nor would the women of the chorus of *Hekabe* be strangers to it. They are captives, about to head off into a lifetime of systematized rape as slaves of the Greek commanders. They begin the ode by addressing Troy's violated condition, then go back to the night before it all began (875–896/905–926):

You O Troy
will no longer be called one of the unsacked cities.
Such a cloud of Greeks covers you,

3. Letter from Samuel Beckett to Axel Kaun, 1937.

rapes you, spear by spear.
Shorn of your crown of towers.
Stained black with fire.
Sorrow!
I shall not walk your ways again.

Midnight my ruin began.
Supper was over, sweet sleep drifting down,
after songs and dances and sacrifice
my husband lay in our chamber,
his spear on its peg.
He was not watching
for Greek sailors
to come walking into Troy.

I was doing my hair,
I was binding my hair,
staring down into the bottomless lake of my mirror,
before I fell into bed—
a scream cut the town,
a roar swept the street...

There is something very moving in the words "I was doing my hair, I was binding my hair"—image of a woman, a night, a city, a world prior to violation. A fact still innocent of metaphor.

3) Clear moral issue: The moral issue of this play is revenge. Hekabe is a crushed human being in the first half of the play, who raises herself up in the second half through an action of revenge. Revenge brings her to life. Why? Because the world after a world war becomes a simple place. It is divided simply into the dead, who are the majority, and those who have somehow managed not to die, whom we call the living. How they live is not important.

Revenge is a form of desire. It is on the side of things living. What kind of desire is revenge? is a question that remains unresolved for me. After studying this play, which is itself a study of revenge, I don't know whether Euripides means us to think of it as good or evil, redemptive or tawdry. Perhaps he doesn't know.

If you google "revenge" you will encounter several considerable things, including the Avenger's Front Page, a tactical handbook of pranks and mayhem "complete with instructions on how to make the working life of a local 7-11 employee into a living nightmare, might apply to other convenience stores as well." You will also meet RevengeLady.com, who "using the ancient art of revenge to bring humor and happiness back to your life" offers you a Revenge Quiz to discover if revenge is right for you. First question: "Revenge is best described as: a) childish b) demeaning c) unhealthy d) an old and honorable tradition that can help alleviate stress and restore balance." And finally you will meet Revenge Unlimited, an empty black screen that says simply "new site and new shopping cart coming soon."

Perhaps the last detail is the most telling. "New site and new shopping cart coming soon" implies a sweeping away of the old order—not just new stuff to buy but a new sensibility with which to buy it, a new method of pushing your cart up and down the aisles. Equipped with your new cart you will be a new person and shopping will make sense again. The only prerequisite for this transformation is a brief interval of empty black screen, i.e. someone needs to perform the savage clarifying gesture that will sweep away the old shopping cart with its load of false consciousness and bad bargains. Ethically, revenge poses as a tautology; as an action (Revenge Lady would say) that can "restore balance," that returns everything to the way it was before. Of course this is an untruth. Nothing is as it was before, after the screen has gone to black. Darkness lies on the soul. To use Beckett's phrase, "what cowers behind it begins to seep through." With her new shopping cart Hekabe, queen of Troy, will be prowling the aisles for dog biscuits.

CAST OF CHARACTERS
In order of appearance

POLYDOROS, *son of Hekabe and a ghost*
HEKABE, *queen of Troy*
CHORUS *of Trojan (female) prisoners of war*
POLYXENA, *daughter of Hekabe*
ODYSSEUS, *a Greek captain*
TALTHYBIOS, *messenger of the Greek army*
(FEMALE) SERVANT *of Hekabe*
AGAMEMNON, *a Greek general*
SOLDIERS *of Agamemnon*
POLYMESTOR, *local Thracian king and guestfriend of Hekabe*
SONS *of Polymestor (mute)*

The scene is set at the encampment of the Greek army on the shore of Thrace, in front of the tents of the Trojan captives, soon after the fall of Troy. There are two side entrances and a central stage building representing the tent of Hekabe.

[enter Polydoros from side entrance]

GHOST OF POLYDOROS

I come from the hidden places of the dead and the
    shadowgates
where Hades lives aloof from other gods.
I am Polydoros,
son of Hekabe
and of Priam.
When Troy was at risk of falling to the Greek spear,
Priam feared for me and sent me out
to the house of his ally in Thrace—
to Polymestor, who rules the Thracian plain.
He sent a lot of gold with me   10
so that, if Troy should fall,
his sons who survived would not live in want.
I was the youngest—too young to carry weapons.
And so long as our boundaries held
and the towers of Troy were unsmashed
and Hektor my brother worked his brilliant spear,
I lived well in the Thracian's house.
Flourished like a sapling—poor sapling!

But when Troy perished,
and Hektor perished,   20
and my father's hearth was razed to the ground
and my father himself slaughtered at the gods' altar
by Achilles' bloodyminded son,
then Polymestor cut me down
to get the gold—
that guestfriend of my father—tossed me in the sea
and kept the gold for himself.

So here I lie,
washing up on the beach, washing back in the waves,
ebbing and flowing,   30
unwept, unburied—
or leave my body vacant
and glide above my mother Hekabe.
Three days I am hovering here,
over my poor mother,
who has come this far
on her way from Troy.
Meanwhile the Greeks all sit by their ships on the shore
    of Thrace.
For Achilles made an appearance above his own tomb
to stop the Greek army from shipping for home.   40
He wants a sacrifice:
he wants my sister Polyxena.
Her blood to honor him.
And he will get this—not go ungifted, not Achilles.
How they love him!

Her fate brings my sister to death on this day.
Two children, two corpses, shall my mother see,

mine and my sister's.
Yes I will show myself—I must get burial!—
some slave will find me here in the waves.   50
I asked this from the powers below,
to find burial and the hands of my mother.
What I wished for I'll have.
But here comes Hekabe, I shall withdraw.
She comes from Agamemnon's tent
in a state of terror.
PHEU! [cry]
O mother! you went from a house of kings to a day of slavery.
Your grief is as great as your splendor was:
some god is weighing the one out equal to the other.   60

[exit Polydoros by side entrance]

[enter Hekabe from tent]

HEKABE

Help her, O children, help the old woman out of the house.
Lead her, set her upright,
O women of Troy—
your fellow slave.
Once a queen.
Bring,
    guide,
        lead,
            lift me,
take hold of my old woman's hand.   70
And I,
leaning on the curve of someone's arm,
shall press my slow foot forward.

Hekabe

O lightning of Zeus, O shadowy Night,
why am I pricked by panic in the darkness—
by phantoms?
O goddess under the earth,
mother of blackwinged dreams,
I drive away the vision that comes by night—
this vision of my son gone to Thrace,   80
this vision of dear Polyxena.
Dread sight. I saw it. I knew!
O gods below, save my son!
He is the one sole anchor of my house,
safe where he is in snowy Thrace,
in the house of his father's guestfriend.
      But something new and strange is at hand.
            Something that smells of *lament*.
      Never before
does my brain shake like this.   90
O Trojan women!
where can I find those sacred souls—Helenos or Kassandra?
Will they help me read my dreams?
For I saw
a little dappled deer being pulled to bits in the bloody claws of
      a wolf.
Pulled from my knees, O pity!
Now terror is on me.
Achilles' ghost showed itself high on his tomb,
demanding a prize.
He wants a Trojan.   100
O gods! send,
      send away,
            send away from my child

this fate,
I pray!

[enter chorus from side entrances]

CHORUS (*entrance song*)
    Hekabe,
    in haste I come to you
    from my master's tent,
    where my lot was cast and my place assigned as a slave.
    I was marched out of Troy at the point of a spear,   110
    caught like an animal,
    caught by Greeks.
    Not in the hope I can lighten your grief,
    but with a burden of news for you,
    O lady: I come as herald of pain.
    In full assembly of the Greeks, they say, it was decided,
    your child will be given in sacrifice to Achilles.
    You know he showed himself,
    mounting his own tomb in solid gold armor,
    and stayed the ships.   120
    He barked at them:
    "Where are you off to, Greeks, leaving my tomb unhonored?"
    Waves of dissent broke over the army.
    Opinions ran through them—some said yes to the sacrifice,
    some said no.
    Agamemnon it was
    who urged your interests,
    loyal as he is to the prophetic girl—
    your daughter Kassandra—or at least to her bed.
    Then the sons of Theseus made two declarations: 130

that the tomb of Achilles be crowned with fresh blood,
that the spear of Achilles not rank second to Kassandra's bed.
Words were tight on both sides
until the old dazzler got up—
that crowdpleasing, honeytalking, wordchopping Odysseus.
He convinced the army not to deny
the best of all the Greeks
for the sake of a slave's sacrifice,
not to let a single dead soul down below
claim that Greeks are ungrateful to Greeks   140
who died on the plain of Troy.

And Odysseus is on his way here now,
any minute now,
to drag the young colt away from your breast,
away from your poor old hands.
Go to the temples,
   go to the altars,
      bend as a suppliant at the knees of Agamemnon.
      Call on the gods of the sky
   and the gods underground.   150
Surely prayers will spare your child!
Or you will have to watch
   her
      fall forward
         at the tomb
            and spray red blood
      from a blackbright hole
as it opens her throat wide.

HEKABE
   IO EGO MELEA! [*cry*] What shall I cry?

What howl shall I howl?
> Wretched in my poor wretched old age,
>> in my poor wretched slavery—it is not endurable!
>>>> it is not bearable!
>>> OIMOI! [*cry*]
>>> Who defends me? What kinsman?
>>> What city? Vanished is the old man,
>> vanished are the children.
> Where shall I go?
Where shall I send me?
Where is there a god or creature who will help?   170
O you Trojan women who bring in evil grief to me,
> you have destroyed me, destroyed me.
Life in the light is no longer a possibility.
> Take me, poor foot,
>> take the poor old woman,
>>> to that tent.
>>> O child! O little one!
>>> your mother's heart breaks—come out! Come out!
>>> Hear me!

[enter Polyxena from tent]

POLYXENA
> IO! [*cry*]   180
> Mother!
> Why are you shouting?
> What news do you bring that shakes me from the tent like a
> fearful bird?

HEKABE
> O child.

POLYXENA

That sounds unlucky. I don't like how you start.

HEKABE

OIMOI! [*cry*] Alas for your life.

POLYXENA

Speak it out!
Panic—mother, why do you groan?

HEKABE

O child, child, your poor mother—

POLYXENA

What? What is your news?   190

HEKABE

Kill. You. Greeks. Achilles' tomb.

POLYXENA

OIMOI! [*cry*] Mother! How can you utter
horrors of evil? Explain to me, explain!

HEKABE

I will tell, child, a tale bad to tell.
The Greeks took a vote to decide your life—
              your dear darling life!

POLYXENA

O you suffering one! You marrow of grief,
              O mother of sadness!
What kind of hostile unspeakable outrage is this

driven against you by a god?   200
   No longer shall I care for you,
      in your bitter old age
         in your bitter slavery,
            I shall not share it.
               No. You will see me,
         like a mountain animal,
        bitter little animal,
      ripped from your hand—
   and my throat cut!
Down to the blackness below   210
where corpses lie—
I shall lie!
O!
You poor mother of mine,
     I weep
        for your endless tears.
          Not for my life, not for my pain, not for my outrage
       do I weep.
       No.
       For you.   220
   To die is lucky.

CHORUS

   Here comes Odysseus hurrying, Hekabe, towards you.

[enter Odysseus from side entrance]

ODYSSEUS

   Woman! I think you're aware of the judgment of the army
   and how the vote went. Nonetheless I'll declaim.
   The Greeks are resolved to slaughter your Polyxena

on top of Achilles' tomb.
They designate me to escort the girl.
As priest in charge of sacrifice, Achilles' son is named.
I assume you know what to do?
Don't make me tear her away by force,   230
don't fight me.
Realize your strength, realize your condition.
You're smart. Think *necessity*.

HEKABE

AIAI! [*cry*] Ah here it is then. Here is my agony.
No lack of groaning. No lack of tears.
I am someone who did not die when I should have died.
Zeus failed to destroy me—he keeps me going!
so I can witness more evils, worse evils
than ever before.
Yet if it is possible   240
for slaves to question free men—
not abrasive questions, not sharp—
can we ask, and you answer, a few things?

ODYSSEUS

Yes. Ask away. I grudge you not.

HEKABE

Remember that night you came as a spy into Troy,
in filthy rags with blood dripping off your chin?

ODYSSEUS

I do. It left its mark on me.

HEKABE

> And Helen recognized you and told no one but me?

ODYSSEUS

> Yes I recall—great danger I was in.

HEKABE

> And you bent low and clasped my knees? 250

ODYSSEUS

> So that my hand all but died away in your robe.

HEKABE

> Then I saved you and sent you from the land?

ODYSSEUS

> Yes. And so I look upon this daylight now.

HEKABE

> And what did you say when you were at my mercy then?

ODYSSEUS

> Anything I could think up, to avoid dying.

HEKABE

> And are you not, then, despicable?
> You had, you admit, good treatment from me.
> Yet you do me no favors, in fact, the greatest conceivable
>> harm!
> Thankless breed, you demagogues!

I curse the knowing of you.   260
You ruin friends lightly,
so long as it helps you please your constituency.
And what clever policy of yours was it
led them to vote against my child?
What necessity drew them on to human slaughter
at a tomb where killing oxen is more suitable?
Or is it as an act of retribution
that Achilles marks out murder for this girl?
But she's done him no wrong.
He ought to ask for Helen!   270
It was Helen who destroyed him,
it was Helen who brought him to Troy.
If a captive needs to die, some woman of incomparable
    loveliness—
don't look at us! Helen is the famous beauty!
And he is her victim!
So far as justice goes, this is my argument.
Now let me tell you what you owe me.
You touched my hand once—you confess—
you touched my face and fell on the ground before me.
So I touch you. I do the same.   280
I claim your gratitude.
I supplicate you:
do not rip the child from my hands.
Do not kill her.
Enough death!
This one is my joy. This one is my forgetting of evils.
She comforts my soul—
she is my city, my walking stick, my way on the road.
I advise you,
beware of wanton power.   290

You may not always be on top.
I was once. Look at me now.
One day took a world away.
By your beard I entreat you, feel shame before me.
Feel pity!
Go to the Greek army,
persuade them.
It doesn't look good to kill women.
Don't you people have the one same law of bloodshed
for free men and slaves?   300
Persuade them, your prestige can do it—
you're a big man, your word has power!

CHORUS

No human nature is so hard
as to hear your groans and long laments
without a tear.

ODYSSEUS

Hekabe, take a lesson.
And do not, in your passion, harden your mind against good
    counsel.
I am, on the one hand, perfectly prepared to save your skin.
You saved mine.
On the other hand,   310
I do not stand down from the recommendation I gave,
now that Troy is captured by the best man in the army,
to slaughter your child.
Because he asks it.
You know, this is how cities go wrong:
when someone brave and ready of heart
wins no more glory than inferior men.

In our eyes Achilles is worth honoring.
He died for Greece, what a beauty of a man!
Would it not be shameful   320
to use him as a friend when he's alive
but turn against him after death?
Of course it would!
What will people say if we ever gather for war again?
They'll say,
Well, shall we fight or love our lives,
seeing the dead get no honor?
Now me, no matter how meager my life from day to day,
I'm satisfied—
so long as I see my tomb decorated as it deserves.   330
That grace lasts a long time.
So you say your sufferings are piteous.
Listen to me,
there are agonies on our side too.
Old women, old men,
young brides torn from husbands.
Dusts of Troy cover them.
Endure it. We all do.
But if we forget how to honor the brave,
we'll be called thugs. And rightly.   340
You barbarians don't know how to treat your friends as friends,
how to venerate men who die beautiful deaths.
The result is: Greece on top!
And your fate matches your policy.

CHORUS
    AIAI! [*cry*] A slave puts up with things that aren't right—
        forced to.

HEKABE

> O daughter, my words for your murder go into the air,
>> pointless.
> But you, if you have any power more than a mother has,
> now is the time—let loose your nightingale's wail—
> so your life be not torn from you!
> Fall at Odysseus' knee,   350
> persuade him. You have a claim!
> Yes he has children himself—he may pity your luck!

POLYXENA

> I see you, Odysseus,
> how you hide your right hand in your cloak,
> how you turn your face away.
> Afraid I'll supplicate?
> Don't worry.
> You're safe.
> I will go with you.
> Because it is necessary.   360
> And because I want to die.
> Unwilling—I'd look like a coward.
> Like a woman in love with her life.
> But why live?
> My father was absolute ruler of all the Trojans,
> that's the first fact of my life.
> Then I was brought up to be a bride of kings—
> it was no small competition—
> oh I queened it among the ladies of Ida!
> How they gazed at me!   370
> I was equal to gods, except for the mortal part.
> So now I'm a slave.

That word—as soon as I hear it
I want to be dead, so strange it is.
And I'll probably get a raw-minded master,
whoever throws down some silver—for me, sister of Hektor!
Yes I'll make his bread and sweep his floor
and stand at the loom, perforce!
Bitter day.
And some slave will sully my bed—   380
I who was good enough for royalty!
No.
I renounce this light of free eyes.
I consign myself to death.
Lead the way, Odysseus. Finish me off.
For I see no reason to hope or imagine good days anymore.
Mother, don't get in my way
by word or deed.
Join me in preferring death to degradation.
For a person unaccustomed to it,   390
the yoke hurts the neck.
Death would be luckier.
To live in an ignoble way is simply pain.

CHORUS

Good breeding is an impressive thing,
not just a word.

HEKABE

Grandly spoken, daughter, but your grandeur brings grief.
Look here, Odysseus,
if you have to gratify Achilles and avoid reproach yourself,
take *me* to his pyre—
stab *me* to death!   400

I am the one who gave birth to Paris—
and Paris who shot Achilles down with his bow!

ODYSSEUS

Not you, old woman,
Achilles wants her.

HEKABE

Then slay me at her side.
Twice as much blood tricking down to the greedy dead.

ODYSSEUS

The girl's death is enough. No need for more.
I wish we didn't owe this!

HEKABE

I must die with my daughter.

ODYSSEUS

Must? You're giving the orders now?   410

HEKABE

As ivy to oak, so shall I cling to her.

ODYSSEUS

Think again.

HEKABE

I will not let her go.

ODYSSEUS

Nor I depart without her.

POLYXENA

Mother, listen to me.
And you, son of Laertes, relax. A parent has a right to rage.
But O my poor mother, don't fight with our masters.
Do you want to be thrown to the ground,
to have your old flesh forced and dragged and wounded,
to be put to shame by strong young arms?   420
No, please. It is unworthy.
O my beloved mother, give me your sweet hand,
lay your cheek on my cheek.
Never again, never again
shall I look on the light of the sun.
Accept this last utterance.
O mother who bore me, I am going below.

HEKABE

O daughter, I shall live as a slave in the light of day.

POLYXENA

No wedding, no bridegroom, these things I deserved.

HEKABE

You are piteous, child, and I a woman broken.   430

POLYXENA

I shall lie there in Hades apart from you.

HEKABE

OIMOI! [*cry*] What shall I do, where end my life?

POLYXENA

As a slave I die, though my father was free.

HEKABE

I had fifty sons, now nothing at all.

POLYXENA

What word shall I say to Hektor your son, to Priam your
husband?

HEKABE

Tell them I am the most sorrowful woman alive.

POLYXENA

O breasts that fed me.

HEKABE

O poor dear daughter, dead before your time.

POLYXENA

Farewell, mother, farewell, Kassandra.

HEKABE

"Farewell" is for others—not for a mother!   440

POLYXENA

And to my brother in Thrace, Polydoros, farewell.

HEKABE

If he lives. I am doubtful. My luck nowadays is not good.

POLYXENA

He does live. And will come to close your eyes when you die.

HEKABE

I am dead before death, from pressure of evil.

POLYXENA

Come, Odysseus. Cover my head. Lead me away.
Before my own death
I have melted my heart
with the cries of my mother,
and my cries melt her.
O light! Yes I call on you—   450
you still belong to me
while I go
between the sword and pyre of Achilles.

HEKABE

OI'GO! [*cry*] I faint. My limbs are loosed.
O daughter, touch your mother, reach out your hand.
Please! Don't leave me childless! I am destroyed.
Just so, destroyed,
would I like to see Spartan Helen,
that one who brought Troy to the dirt
with her beautiful eyes.   460

[*exit Polyxena and Odysseus by side entrance*]

CHORUS (*first choral ode*)
Breeze, breeze of the sea,
calling quick ships over the open ocean,
where will you take me, hopeless as I am?
What house will get me as its slave?
Where will I end up—some Dorian anchor?

or some place in Phthia, where they say
the streams of Apidanos make the plains glitter?

Or shall I go on a seasweeping oar
to a house of bitter days
on that island where the date palm   470
and the bay tree first held up their holy branches
to honor Leto in her travail?
Shall I sing with the girls of Delos
for Artemis of the golden veil and the golden bow?

Or shall I yoke up horses in Athens,
embroidering them on a yellow robe
in intricate flowerworked webs?
Or perhaps the race of Titans
that Zeus put to sleep with a bolt of fire?

Alas for my children, my father, my land—   480
fallen, ruined, smoldering, spearcaught.
I shall be "slave" in a foreign land,
leave Asia behind,
change to a bedroom in hell.

[enter Talthybios by side entrance]

TALTHYBIOS
Where can I find the queen of Troy?

CHORUS
Right there on her back on the ground,
Talthybios, shut in her robes.

TALTHYBIOS

Zeus! what can I say—that you watch over human beings?
that you care mortal luck?
Or is it a delusion we persist in?   490
Is this woman not queen of the Trojans and all their gold?
Is this woman not wife of fabulous Priam?
But now her city is torn up by spears,
she herself a slave, ancient, childless, flat on the ground,
fouling her poor head in the dirt.
PHEU PHEU! [*cry*] I too am old. But let me die before I
   fall into shame.
Rise, poor one, lift your body and your old white head.

HEKABE

EA! [*cry*] Leave me be. Who is this who won't let me lie on the
   ground?
Why do you bother me? I am in pain.

TALTHYBIOS

I am Talthybios. I serve the Greeks.   500
Sent by Agamemnon, woman.

HEKABE

O blessed friend! Are you come from the Greeks to slay me too?
Welcome news!
Let's go, let's get on with it, lead the way, old man.

TALTHYBIOS

So that you may bury your child who is dead, woman,
I came in search of you.
The Atreidai sent me and the Greek people.

HEKABE

OIMOI! [*cry*] What do you say? I am not to die?
You are here with more evils?
O my child, my dead child, torn from your mother.   510
So I lose you.
Here is grief.
And how did you slay her?
Were you respectful—
or did you go at her dreadfully like an enemy?
Tell me, though the words be not kind.

TALTHYBIOS

You want to win double tears from me, woman.
Telling it I will weep again as I did at the tomb where she died.
The army was massed in front of the tomb for the slaughter.
Then the son of Achilles took Polyxena by the hand,   520
stood her on top of the mound (and I nearby).
Certain chosen young men were in attendance
to curb the wild leaping of your little calf.
And taking a full gold cup in his hands
Achilles' son pours libation to his father.
He signals me to proclaim silence to the army.
I took my position and said in their midst:
"Silence, Achaians! Let the whole host be still!
Keep silence!" Breathless they stood.
He spoke: 530
"O Achilles, my father,
receive these poured offerings, peace offerings
to call up the dead. Come!
Drink the black blood of a girl inviolate—
that is our gift to you, mine and the army's.
Be gracious to us,

loose the ships and the cables,
grant us all our homecoming from Troy."
So he spoke.
All the army together joined in his prayer.   540
Then he took his gold sword out of its sheath.
Nodded to the young men to seize the girl.
But she—very aware—spoke out:
"Greeks! You who razed my city!
It is my will to die. Let no one touch my skin!
I shall offer my throat in good courage.
But let me stand free—I would die free!—for gods' sake,
      while you kill me.
Among the dead to be called a slave when I am a queen
      shames me!"
Then the men roared "Yes!" and king Agamemnon said to let
      the girl go.
When she heard the command she took her robe at the
      shoulderpoint   550
and tore it all the way to the navel.
Exposed her breasts beautiful as a statue.
Set her knee on the ground and spoke to all a word of
      absolute nerve:
"Here! if you want to strike the chest, young man, strike!
Or if you want the neck, I turn my throat to you!"
And he, pitying the girl, cuts her breath in two.
Red shoots forth.
Yet as she died, even so,
she thought how to fall,
how to hide what must be hidden from the eyes of men.   560
And when she'd paid her life out in that slaughter
all the Greeks set to work.
Some poured leaves on the dead girl,

some heaped the pyre with pine wood,
everyone not working heard this rebuke:
"Do you stand idle, you worthless man,
with nothing in your hands for the girl?
Will you offer no tribute to her high heart,
to her extraordinary soul?"
Such is my story of your dead child,   570
O most blessed, and most unlucky
of all mothers, as I see.

CHORUS

A dreadful thing has boiled up over Priam
and his city. Here is gods' necessity.

HEKABE

O daughter, I don't know what evil to look at,
so many are here. If I take hold of one,
another pushes in, then some other sorrow on that side—
grief on grief!
And now your agony—
how can I wipe it from my mind?   580
Yet it lightens me—this report of your greatness.
Is it not strange
that a bad ground blessed with good weather will bring forth
    good crop,
and good soil deprived of what it needs gives bad fruit,
but with human beings
a scoundrel produces a scoundrel every time,
and a good man a good man.
Adverse conditions do not spoil a decent human nature.
Still I wonder is it parents or teaching makes the difference?
Every good upbringing involves teaching.   590

Hekabe

But my mind wanders.
You [*to Talthybios*]—go tell Agamemnon
no one touches my daughter.
Keep that mob back.
In a big army
there is something anarchic, worse than fire, unpredictable.

[exit Talthybios by side entrance]

You, old servant, take a jar,
fill it with seawater and bring it back here.
So I may give my child her last bath—
maiden nonmaiden, bride nonbride.   600
Can I lay her out as she deserves?
No impossible.
But I'll use what I have: get some pretty things from the
     captive women—
someone may have tucked away a bit of treasure.

[exit female Servant]

O forms of home, O once prosperous houses,
O rich prolific Priam and I myself, aged mother of your
     children,
what nothing we are!
Zero!
Look how people get puffed up,
one for his wealthy home,   610
one for his fame in the city—
these things are null, vanity, wishful thinking, boasts of the
     tongue.

That man is blessed
on whom day by day evil does not fall.

[exit Hekabe into tent]

CHORUS (*second choral ode*)

It was ordained for me—catastrophe.
It was ordained for me—grief.
When Paris
cut the pines of Ida
and sailed the sea to Helen's bed—
most lovely of all the women on whom the sun gazes.   620

Works of war unroll around us,
and necessities worse than the works of war.
Out of private folly
a national evil for the Trojan land—
deadliness from strangers.
It came from a shepherd to three goddesses on Ida,

a judgment of war and death and outrage.
By the river Eurotas
someone is groaning in tears for her house,
some old mother is putting her hand up   630
to drag bloody lines in her cheek.

[enter female Servant]

SERVANT

Women, where is the all-suffering Hekabe
who surpasses every human being in evils?
No one shall rob her of this crown.

CHORUS

Why? What now?
Do announcements of grief never sleep?

SERVANT

I bring Hekabe pain.
Evils all around. Not easy to say something happy.

CHORUS

Here she is out from the house
to meet your words.   640

[enter Hekabe from tent]

SERVANT

O queen of affliction!
More than I can say.
You are lost, nonexistent, though your eyes are open—
childless, manless, cityless, ruined woman.

HEKABE

This is not news.
You taunt me!
But why are you bringing a corpse?—Polyxena's?—
they told me her burial would be done by the Greeks.

SERVANT

She knows nothing, bewails Polyxena.
Of new sorrows she has no grasp.   650

HEKABE

No! Surely it is not Kassandra's
head you bring?

SERVANT

Kassandra is alive. This one here is dead—
but you do not bewail him.
Look at the corpse. Prepare yourself.

HEKABE

OIMOI! [*cry*] I look upon my own child dead!
Polydoros—but the Thracian was keeping him safe!
I am lost.
Annihilated.
O child,   660
AIAI! [*cry*] There are cries, I begin the cries.
Ugly tune taught by an avenging god.

SERVANT

You recognize your child, O poor woman.

HEKABE

Unbelievable, strange, strange, unbelievable, I see it.
Evils come pouring over evils.
Never will a day without groaning, a day without tears
reach me.

CHORUS

Evils, O sad woman.

HEKABE

O child, child of a miserable mother,

by what fate did you die, 670
in what doom do you lie,
by whose hand?

SERVANT

I don't know. I found him on the shore.

HEKABE

A thrown out thing! In a fall of blood or on the smooth sand?

SERVANT

Breaking waves carried him from the sea.

HEKABE

OIMOI AIAI! [*cry*] I was not wrong.
That vision of eyes, that blackwinged shape was no mistake:
I saw you, poor child, no longer alive in the daylight of Zeus.

CHORUS

Who killed him? Since you are dream minded, can you say?

HEKABE

It was my friend, my good guestfriend, 680
the Thracian,
the charioteer,
in the house where his old father put him to hide.

CHORUS

OIMOI [*cry*] What do you mean? He was killed for gold?

HEKABE

Things not to be said, not to be named, beyond amazement,

unholy, unbearable!
Where is the justice of host and guest?
O accursed of men! How you did rend his flesh,
how you did chop the limbs of this child
with an iron blade and you had no pity!   690

CHORUS

O sad one.
Some heavy god has put more pain on you than any other
    human being.
But here, I see the form of Agamemnon coming.
Silence, women.

[enter Agamemnon from side entrance]

AGAMEMNON

Hekabe, why delay putting your child in a grave?
Talthybios instructed me none of the Greeks was to touch her.
We let her lie. We handle her not.
Yet you are surprisingly slow.
I come to hurry you.
All the details are well and good—   700
if "well and good" can apply to situations like this.
Ha! who is this man I see by your tent,
a dead Trojan? By the cloth he's wrapped in,
he is no Greek.

HEKABE

Wretch!—myself I mean, Hekabe I am talking to you,
what shall I do? Fall at the knee of Agamemnon here?
Or bear it in silence?

AGAMEMNON

Why do you turn your back to my face and lament?
Tell me what happened, who is this man?

HEKABE

But suppose he thrusts me from his knees as an enemy
slave—more pain!   710

AGAMEMNON

I am no prophet. I can't read you.

HEKABE

How to calculate the mind of this man?
Is he an enemy? How much of an enemy?

AGAMEMNON

Look, if you want me kept in the dark
that's fine: I've no wish to hear it.

HEKABE

But I cannot avenge my children without his help.
Why do I turn it over and over?
I must bite down, whether I win or lose—
Agamemnon, I supplicate you
by your knees and your chin and your happy right hand.   720

AGAMEMNON

Seeking what? Your freedom? That is easily granted.

HEKABE

No, no. Revenge is what I want—
I'd slave my whole life for it!

AGAMEMNON

What help are you asking of me?

HEKABE

Nothing you expect.
You see this corpse on which I drop my tears?

AGAMEMNON

I do. And so?

HEKABE

I gave him birth, I carried him.

AGAMEMNON

Which of your sons is this, sad woman?

HEKABE

Not one of Priam's, who were killed beneath Troy.   730

AGAMEMNON

You bore another son?

HEKABE

Pointlessly, it seems. Here he lies.

AGAMEMNON

But where was he when the city fell?

HEKABE

His father sent him out to save his life.

AGAMEMNON
Sent him out where?

HEKABE
To this land of Thrace where now he is a corpse.

AGAMEMNON
To Polymestor? To the ruler of the land?

HEKABE
Yes. Sent in the care of some very bitter gold.

AGAMEMNON
Who killed him? How?

HEKABE
Who else? My friend the Thracian.   740

AGAMEMNON
O pitiless man! He wanted the gold?

HEKABE
As soon as he knew of Troy's doom.

AGAMEMNON
Where did you find the body? Or did someone bring it?

HEKABE
This servant: found him on the shore.

AGAMEMNON
Was she searching for him?

HEKABE

No, she went for seawater to bathe Polyxena.

AGAMEMNON

Your guestfriend, it seems, killed him, then threw the body out.

HEKABE

A sea-thrashed thing. And look how he hacked up the flesh.

AGAMEMNON

O poor woman. There is no measure to your evils.   750

HEKABE

I do not exist. There is nothing left. Not even evils.

AGAMEMNON

PHEU PHEU! [*cry*] I do pity you! What woman has had
    luck as bad as this?

HEKABE

None save Luck herself.
But hear why I am supplicating you.
If you think my sufferings suit some divine law,
I shall acquiesce.
But if not,
become my avenger on this man,
this utterly unholy guestfriend
and his utterly unholy deed,
for he has no fear of those below the earth or those above.   760
Oftentimes he sat at my table,
was counted first of my friends,
enjoyed his due.

And he watched his chance to commit murder.
Then didn't even think the body worthy of a grave!
Just threw it in the sea.
Well I am a slave and perhaps I'm weak.
But the gods are strong. So is the law that rules the gods.
By reason of this law we believe in gods
and live our lives distinguishing right from wrong.   770
If you flout this law now,
if men go unpunished who murder guests,
who dare to violate the holy things of gods,
then there is no justice among human beings.
Call this shameful! Respect me!—
and take pity.
Or else stand back like a painter and contemplate me,
the evils I suffer.
Once I was royal power. Now your slave.
Once I bloomed with children.   780
Now old, childless, cityless, nullified. Nothing.
OIMOI TALAINA! [*cry*] Ha! where are you slinking off to?
Oh this is futile. I am lost.
Why is it people toil at every other kind of goal
but the study of Persuasion—
this goddess who tyrannizes men—
we could learn to persuade others,
we could get what we want!
How does anyone hope to succeed?
My children are no more.   790
Myself a prisoner of war.
Shame inside me, shame all around me.
Lost.
Look at the smoke there rising over Troy.
And yet:

probably pointless to try an erotic tactic—still, why not.
My daughter sleeps with you, the one the Trojans call
    Kassandra.
What will you give for those nights of love?
For those fond embraces,
what return shall my child have,   800
or me?
Out of the dark, out of love in the night,
come all our greatest grace and gratitude.
Hear this now. You see that dead boy?
If you do well by him, you'll honor your bond with
    Kassandra.
I have only one sentence left.
I want a voice
put into my arms and hands and hair and feet
by some magic of God, so they can all cling to you
and cry out in supplication,   810
cry out every word there is!
O master, O supreme light of the Greeks,
give way to me,
offer your hand to an old woman
who needs an avenger.
She may be nothing. Do it still.
It marks a good man to serve justice
and to hit evil with evil everywhere.

CHORUS

    Strange how mortal events converge.
    Necessity defines us,   820
    making friends of our worst enemies
    and enemies of those who served us well.

AGAMEMNON

    I pity you Hekabe, and your son and your luck and your
        suppliant hand.

    As far as gods and justice go,

    I want to give you vengeance on that unholy guestfriend—

    at least if I can avoid looking (in the eyes of the army)

    like I'm conniving at a Thracian's death

    for the sake of Kassandra.

    Here is where it gets complicated:

    the army holds this Thracian man a friend   830

    and your dead son its enemy.

    You love your son—that's no concern of the army.

    Think of it this way: you have me willing to join your side—

    I'm quick to help.

    But slow, if the army disapproves.

HEKABE

    PHEU! [*cry*] Shit.

    No mortal exists who is free.

    Slaves to money or fortune or the city mob or the written
        laws—

    none use their own mind!

    Since you so dread and overrate your army,   840

    I set you free from this fear.

    Take this thought: if I plot any evil for the killer of my son,

    you need not share the deed.

    But if any violence or rescue attempt arises from the Greeks,

    when this Thracian suffers what he shall suffer,

    suppress it. Without seeming to do so for my sake.

    All the rest—trust me—will go fine.

AGAMEMNON

How? What will you do? Sword? Poison?
Who will help? Where are your friends?

IIEKABE

These tents hide Trojan women.   850

AGAMEMNON

You mean the prisoners of the Greeks?

HEKABE

With them I shall take vengeance on my murderer.

AGAMEMNON

And how can women prevail over men?

HEKABE

There's a strange power, bad power, in numbers combined with
    cunning.

AGAMEMNON

Strange indeed. But I am skeptical.

HEKABE

Why? Didn't women wipe out the sons of Aigyptos?
Didn't women depopulate Lemnos of men?
So it will be. That's enough talk.
Send this servant safely through the lines.
You [*to Servant*] pay a visit to our Thracian guestfriend.   860
Say: Hekabe, former queen of Troy, invites you.
On business no less yours than hers.
And bring your sons, they need to hear it too.

[exit Servant]

Now [*turning*] hold off, Agamemnon,
the burial of freshkilled Polyxena.
I want these two,
brother and sister—twice a mother's agony!—
to lie side by side in the ground.

AGAMEMNON
    So it will be.
    If the army had sailing, I couldn't give you this grace.   870
    But as things are, God sends no wind, and we must wait
      and watch.
    Somehow, I hope, it will all turn out well in the end.
    This is common to men and cities—
    to hope that evil will falter and decency win.

[exit Agamemnon by side entrance]

CHORUS (*third choral ode*)
          You O Troy
    will no longer be called one of the unsacked cities.
       Such a cloud of Greeks covers you,
          rapes you, spear by spear.
       Shorn of your crown of towers.
         Stained black with fire.   880
          Sorrow!
       I shall not walk your ways again.

        Midnight my ruin began.
    Supper was over, sweet sleep drifting down,

after songs and dances and sacrifice
my husband lay in our chamber,
his spear on its peg.
He was not watching
for Greek sailors
to come walking into Troy.   890

I was doing my hair,
I was binding my hair,
staring down into the bottomless lake of my mirror,
before I fell into bed—
a scream cut the town,
a roar swept the street:
O sons of Greece, will you ever take
the tower of Troy
and see your homes again?

I left my bed in just a robe   900
like a Spartan girl
to supplicate holy Artemis. Useless! Sorrow!
I saw my husband killed.
They drove me down
to the salt sea.
Then I looked back as the ship set sail,
pulling me further and further from Troy
and I fainted away.

Helen I cursed!
Paris I cursed!   910
Wasted my land,
emptied my home—

that marriage that was no marriage,
but some spirit of bloodvengeance crying grief down on us.
May she never cross the sea again.
May she never see her home.

[enter Polymestor with Sons from side entrance]

POLYMESTOR

O Priam, dearest of men, and you, dearest Hekabe!
I weep to see you and your city
and your recently dead daughter.
PHEU! [*cry*],   920
one can trust nothing. Not one's good name,
not one's good fortune—it may all turn bad.
The gods themselves confound things,
make chaos of our lives,
so that in ignorance we'll worship them.
But why lament this?
We can never get ahead of evils.
Now you, if you've any reproach to make because of my
       absence,
hold it. For as it happened
I was off in mid-Thrace when you came here.   930
No sooner I got back
than I set out again
and met your servant
and here I am.

HEKABE

I am ashamed to face you, Polymestor,
in this disgusting condition.
You have seen me brilliant!

Now brought so low
I find it hard to look you in the eye.
Don't take it personally.   940
Anyway, it's not our custom
for women to confront men straight.

POLYMESTOR

Well of course not. Now why do you need me?
Why did you bring me from home?

HEKABE

I want to confide a private matter
to you and your sons. Bid your men withdraw.

POLYMESTOR

[*to his men*] Go. I am safe here alone.
[*to Hekabe*] You are my friend and the Greek army likes me.
But now explain:
how may a friend who is prospering help one who is not?   950
I am ready.

HEKABE

First tell me of Polydoros,
the child we sent to your house—
is he alive? Other questions come second.

POLYMESTOR

Absolutely, yes. In him you are blessed.

HEKABE

My dearest friend! How good your words, how worthy of you!

POLYMESTOR

What else do you want to know?

HEKABE

Does he still remember me at all?

POLYMESTOR

In fact he sought to come here to you secretly.

HEKABE

And the gold he brought from Troy, is it safe?   960

POLYMESTOR

Safe yes, under guard in my house.

HEKABE

Guard it well. Don't get greedy.

POLYMESTOR

Certainly not. I pray to enjoy my own wealth.

HEKABE

So do you know what I want to say?

POLYMESTOR

No I do not. You were about to explain this.

HEKABE

There are, O beloved friend—you are such a friend to me!—

POLYMESTOR

Yes, yes, but what is it you want me to know?

HEKABE

—ancient vaults of Priam's gold.

POLYMESTOR

You want me to communicate this to your son?

HEKABE

Exactly. Communicate it. You pious man.   970

POLYMESTOR

Why then must my children be here?

HEKABE

In case you die, better they should know too.

POLYMESTOR

Good point, very smart.

HEKABE

Have you heard of the caves of Trojan Athene?

POLYMESTOR

That's where the gold is? What marks the spot?

HEKABE

A black rock rising high off the ground.

POLYMESTOR

Anything else?

HEKABE

Can you keep safe the treasure I brought out of Troy?

POLYMESTOR

Where is it? Inside your robes? Some secret place?

HEKABE

Under a pile of plunder, there in my tent.   980

POLYMESTOR

Where do you mean? Inside the Greek camp?

HEKABE

The tents of the captive women are private.

POLYMESTOR

Inside it's safe? Devoid of men?

HEKABE

No Greeks in there, we women are alone.
Do come inside.
For the Greeks are eager to set sail from Troy.
And as soon as you get everything you deserve,
you can go with your boys
back to the home where you shelter my son.

[exit Polymestor, his Sons, and Hekabe into tent]

CHORUS

You have not paid, but soon you will: your price!   990
Like a man tumbling into foul water
you fall sideways out of your own heart,
you forfeit your life!
Where justice and gods coincide—
deadly evil.

Your hopes will cheat you,
your hopes have led you
to death and hell,
O miserable man.
You will lose your life to a hand that never fought a war.   1000

POLYMESTOR

[*from inside*] OMOI! [*cry*] I am blinded! Light of my eyes!

CHORUS

Did you hear the Thracian scream ladies?

POLYMESTOR

OMOI! [*cry*] Again! O my children! Butchery!

CHORUS

New and strange evils come to pass inside.

POLYMESTOR

You shall not escape!
I'll tear down the walls!

CHORUS

Should we rush in? Help Hekabe? The crisis calls.

[enter Hekabe from tent]

HEKABE

Smash it, spare nothing, pull the place down!
You'll not put sight back into your eyes
nor see your children alive—I have killed them!   1010

CHORUS

Have you mastered the Thracian?
Lady, have you done what you say?

HEKABE

See him now coming out of the house,
a blind man stumbling on blind steps.
And his children, whom I killed,
with the help of the Trojan women.
He has given me justice.
Here he comes, look.
I'll get back out of range.
His fury is fantastic.   1020

[enter Polymestor from tent]

POLYMESTOR

OMOI EGO! [*cry*] Where do I go,
where can I stand,
where take shelter—
hopping along on four feet like a beast of the mountains?
Should I change tack—go this way, go that,
to grab those manslaughtering Trojan women who
    mutilated me?
Miserable miserable women of Troy,
O you accursed women of Troy,
where have you run to?
O Helios   1030
I pray you heal the blind hole of my eye
and change it to light!
A A! [*cry*]
Silence.

I perceive the secret step of women somewhere here.
Which direction shall I go
to leap on them and glut myself with bones and flesh,
make an animal meal of them—
brutality to pay for what they did to me!
O TALAS! [*cry*]   1040
Where am I going, how do I stumble,
bereft of my children,
torn apart by these Bacchants of hell?
Cut to bits and thrown out on the mountains
as a bloody breakfast for the dogs?
Where can I stop,
where can I step,
where can I turn,
gathering my robes as a ship its sails
to rush upon this den of deadly beasts?   1050
To guard my children!

CHORUS

Unhappy man, what unbearable evils you committed.
Degradation is the price you pay.
Yes! the god who gave it is a heavy god.

POLYMESTOR

AIAI IO! [*cry*] O Thrace—
spearbearing horseloving warrior people of Thrace!
IO [*cry*] Greeks! IO [*cry*] sons of Atreus! I cry for help!
Come! Help me! For gods' sake!
Is there anyone who hears?
Is there any who will help?   1060
Why do you delay?
Women destroyed me, women with weapons.

Dreadful, dreadful is my pain.
OMOI! [*cry*] Outrage!
Where can I turn?
Where should I go?
Shall I fly to the roof of heaven
where Orion and Sirios shoot fire from their eyes,
or plunge into the black boat that drives to Hades?

CHORUS

Understandable, if a man in this much pain   1070
should rid himself of life.

[enter Agamemnon with soldiers from side entrance]

AGAMEMNON

At your shout I came.
Echo rang through the camp.
Had we not know Troy was taken,
that din would have moved us to fear.

POLYMESTOR

O dearest friend, it is your voice I hear and know—
Agamemnon, you see my suffering.

AGAMEMNON

EA! [*cry*] Polymestor, wretched man, who has destroyed
   you?
Who has blinded your eyes
and murdered your children? What hatred!   1080

POLYMESTOR

Hekabe.

With her women.
Destroyed me.
Worse than destroyed me.

AGAMEMNON

[*turning*] *You,* Hekabe?
You had the nerve for this?

POLYMESTOR

OMOI [*cry*] What? She is near me?
Show me, tell me where—I'll rip her to bloody pieces with
  my hands!

AGAMEMNON

Here! What are you doing?

POLYMESTOR

By the gods I beg you   1090
let me to go at her!
I have rage in my hands!

AGAMEMNON

No, stop.
Put savagery away.
I will listen to both of you in turn
and judge the cause objectively.

POLYMESTOR

I will speak.
There was a certain Polydoros,
youngest son of Priam and of Hekabe,
whom Priam gave to me to bring up in my home,   1100

anxious as he was about Troy's capture.
This boy I killed. Why did I kill him?
Prudence and foresight.
I had a fear that if this boy—your enemy—survived,
he'd resurrect Troy,
then if the Greeks heard a son of Priam was alive
they'd make a second expedition
and devastate Thrace
and we'd suffer once again
for being neighbors of the Trojans,   1110
as we have in the past.
So when Hekabe learned of her son's doom
she brought me here on the pretext
that she wanted to show me Priam's hidden gold.
Led me into her tent with my children.
Sat me down on a bed.
Hands were around me, all those hands, women's hands,
on the left, on the right, Trojan women
sat by me in a friendly way, praising the cloth of my robe,
holding it up to the light,   1120
others began admiring my Thracian spear,
they had me take it off, stripped me of my weapons.
And all the little mothers were marveling
at my children, fondling them and passing them
hand to hand,
further and further out of the reach of their father.
Then out of a clear sky—picture this!—daggers
appear from their robes and they are stabbing
my sons! They grab my hands and feet.
If I try to lift my head they drag me back by the hair.   1130
If I lift my arm I cannot move against the female mass of
   them.

And at last—agony beyond agony—
they took their brooches and gouged out my eyes,
my poor eyes! Red blood ran down.
Then the women scattered through the house.
I leapt up like an animal to chase those polluted bitches,
bashing and battering everything in my path.
All this I suffered in your interest,
Agamemnon,
because I took your enemy.   1140
But no need for long speeches.
If any man has spoken ill of women
or does so now
or will do so in future,
I sum it up—
neither land nor sea nourishes any other such species!
A man who encounters them knows this.

CHORUS

Don't sweep the whole female species together for
   condemnation
because of your own catastrophe.
We are many—some blameless,   1150
some not.

HEKABE

Agamemnon! It is not right—it never was—
for talk to signify more than action.
Good deeds and good speech should go together,
as bad with bad—you can't disguise the one with the other.
There are slick rhetoricians of course,
but they don't win in the end.
They foul themselves up.

[*to Agamemnon*] This preamble was for you.
Now I'll turn to *him*.   1160
[*to Polymestor*] You say you spared the Greeks a second war
and slew my child for Agamemnon's sake.
In the first place, you piece of absolute evil,
no barbarian ever helped a Greek, nor ever could.
So why were you so zealous?
Was there kinship or a marriage alliance at stake?
Or some other reason?
Were they really going to sail here a second time
and cut down every cornstalk?
Who would believe this?
It was the gold—tell the truth—that killed my son.   1170
The gold, your profit.
Now here's a question:
how is it that, when Troy was flourishing,
when her towers ran solid around the city,
when Priam was alive and Hektor's spear in flower—
and you really wanted to do Agamemnon a favor—
how is it you didn't kill the child then,
in your house, or else bring him alive to the Greeks?
But you waited, didn't you, until our star went black,   1180
until stinking smoke announced our city taken.
It was then you killed the guestfriend at your hearth.
Now here's another proof of your evil:
if you were such a friend to the Greeks
why didn't you give them the gold?
You admit it wasn't yours and they were in desperate need,
living hand to mouth in an alien land.
You can't let it go even now, can you—got it
locked up in your house, right?
But you know,

if you'd kept my child safe as you should have,   1190
people would call you a fine person.
For in bad times good men prove the truest friends.
And if you'd become poor while he was alive,
he would have been a treasure for you.
Well, as things look now, you have no friend,
the gold is gone, the children too,
and you yourself are as you are!
I tell you, Agamemnon,
if you help this man you will show yourself evil—
supporting someone neither pious   1200
nor loyal
nor holy
nor just.
If you condone that, what does it say about you?

CHORUS

PHEU PHEU! [*cry*] Well, good causes are always an
   occasion
for good arguments, aren't they?

AGAMEMNON

Depressing to have to judge the crimes of others—
but necessary. I agreed to this.
So here is my view.
You killed a man who was your guestfriend   1210
not for my sake, nor to help the Greeks,
but to get that gold.
Nimble rhetoric notwithstanding.
Now perhaps with you it's a light thing to kill a guestfriend,
but for Greeks a serious crime.
How can I call you innocent?

I'd lose credibility.
Not possible.
You steeled yourself for atrocious acts.
Now endure atrocity yourself.   1220

POLYMESTOR

OIMOI! [*cry*] It seems I am beaten by a woman,
a slave!
Stepped on by the lowest of the low!

AGAMEMNON

But justly, since you committed crimes?

POLYMESTOR

OIMOI [*cry*] I wail for my children, I wail for my eyes.

HEKABE

You are in pain, so what? What about my pain, my boy?

POLYMESTOR

Enjoy triumphing over me, don't you, you piece of work?

HEKABE

Should I not rejoice to see you punished?

POLYMESTOR

You won't rejoice for long—when the salt sea—

HEKABE

Carries me to Greece?   1230

POLYMESTOR

No—swallows you down as you drop from the mast.

HEKABE

Why? Pushed? By whom?

POLYMESTOR

You'll go up the mast of your own free will.

HEKABE

How? Wings?

POLYMESTOR

You are destined to turn into a dog. With eyes of red fire.

HEKABE

How do you know this?

POLYMESTOR

Dionysos told me, the prophet of Thrace.

HEKABE

Yet he didn't foretell your own catastrophe?

POLYMESTOR

No. If he had, you'd not have trapped me.

HEKABE

Am I to die here or fill out my life?   1240

POLYMESTOR

Die. And your grave will be called—

HEKABE
After my shape?

POLYMESTOR
—*the tomb of the dog*. A landmark for sailors.

HEKABE
Paying you back is my only concern.

POLYMESTOR
And your daughter Kassandra also must die.

HEKABE
I spit on your words. Turn them back on you.

POLYMESTOR
His wife will kill her, bitter in her house.

HEKABE
May she not go so mad!

POLYMESTOR
And him too, when she lifts her axe high.

AGAMEMNON
Are you out of your mind? Asking for trouble?   1250

POLYMESTOR
Kill me. But a bath of blood awaits you in Argos.

AGAMEMNON
[*to soldiers*] Take him away!

POLYMESTOR
> Do I pain you?

AGAMEMNON
> Stop his mouth!

POLYMESTOR
> Gag me, go ahead. The thing is said.

AGAMEMNON
> Take and throw him on a deserted island
> since he wants to run his mouth so much.

[exit Polymestor with soldiers by side entrance]

> Hekabe,
> creature of sorrow, go bury your children.
> Trojan women, 1260
> you must gather to the tents of your masters.
> For I see the winds do start to blow.
> May we sail home safe
> and see all things happy in our houses,
> released as we are, from this ordeal.

[exit Agamemnon by side entrance and Hekabe into tent]

CHORUS
> Go to the harbor, go to the tents, dear women.
> Now we taste the work of slaves.
> Hard is necessity.

HIPPOLYTOS

PREFACE

"The face as the extreme precariousness of the other...." [1]

The *Hippolytos* is like Venice. A system of reflections, distorted reflections, reflections that go awry. A system of corridors where people follow one another but never meet, never find the way out. There is no way out, all corridors lead back into the system. Hippolytos wants to be like Artemis, but even in death he is not allowed to see her face. Phaidra wants to be like Hippolytos, but she has not a single conversation with him in the course of the play. What might such a conversation have changed? What does the face matter? Both Hippolytos and Phaidra systematically avoid certain kinds of precariousness. If you asked Hippolytos to name his system he would say "shame." Oddly, if you asked Phaidra to name her system she would also say "shame." They do not mean the same thing by this word. Or perhaps they do. Too bad they never talk.

Aidos ("shame") is a vast word in Greek. Its lexical equivalents include "awe, reverence, respect, self-respect, shamefastness, sense of honor, sobriety, moderation, regard for others, regard for the helpless, compassion, shyness, coyness, scandal, dignity, majesty, Majesty." Shame vibrates with honor and also with disgrace, with what is chaste and with what is erotic, with coldness and also with blushing. Shame is felt before the eyes of others and also in

1. Emmanuel Levinas, "Peace and Proximity," in *Basic Philosophical Writings*, edited by Adriaan T. Peperzak, Simon Critchley, and Robert Bernasconi (Indiana University Press, 1996), page 167.

facing oneself. To Phaidra most of all, shame is a split emotion. She calls it a pleasure (430ff/385ff)* then divides it into two kinds: one good, one bad. Scholars disagree on what she means by this distinction but it is clear she believes shame of the bad kind can ruin her and that she must nullify it at any cost. For Hippolytos shame is simple. He personifies Shame as the goddess who guards his private meadow of virtue and celebrates her in his opening hymn to Artemis (96–106/73–78):

> For you
>   this crown
>   from a field uncut
> O queen I wove and bring—
> from a virgin field where no shepherd dares to graze his animal,
> no knife comes near it—
>   field uncut,
> just a bee dozing by in spring.
> And Shame
>   waters it with river dews.

Shame is a system of exclusions and purity that subtends Hippolytos' religion. Interesting, then, to notice the presence of a bee within his private religious space. For there is some evidence that the bee, in its role of busy pollinator, was associated with Aphrodite's cult. And you will hear the chorus make a direct comparison between Aphrodite and the bee later in the play, in a choral ode celebrating the unavoidability of Eros (580–636/525–564). So you might begin to wonder about Hippolytos' simplicity. Consider also the fact that *aidos* turns up in Greek lyric poetry as

---

*Please note that the first set of figures given refers to the line numbers of the present translation, the second to those of the Greek text.

a component of sexual pleasure, e.g. in a passage of Pindar where Aphrodite unites two lovers in this way:

> silverfooted Aphrodite
> shed seductive shame/charming coyness (*aidos*)
> on their sweet bed
>
> (Pindar, *Pythian Odes*, 9.12)

And the fact that in epic poetry the word *aidos* is used in the plural (*aidoia*) as a euphemism for the sexual organs (*Iliad*, 2.262). These sexual and erotic strands form only part of the word *aidos*, but it is a part that Hippolytos edits out. He edits Artemis too. Her sexlessness reminds him of his own chastity; he idolizes it. Her prestige as mistress of the hunt coincides with his favorite activity; he makes it a form of worship. Her epithet *parthenos* ("virgin, maiden, girl") is used by him as if it named Artemis to a different species than the female race that he denounces ("this counterfeit thing—woman?" [684ff/616ff]). He seems to want to place Artemis, and himself, in a special third gender—the translucent gender—unpolluted by flesh or change.

But, as the chorus remind us in their entrance song (153ff/121ff), Artemis has much to do with flesh and change. She is, for example, patron goddess of the blood and pain of childbirth, commonly invoked by women in travail. Could Hippolytos admit this aspect of her? Hippolytos' favorite adjective for the Artemis-atmosphere in which he wishes to exist is *akeratos*, "uncut, unharvested, untouched, inviolate, pure, perfect." When he uses *akeratos* of Artemis' meadow he means that the grass is literally "uncut" but there is a reference to sexual purity too. For the adjective could connote virgin intactness, and virgins did cut their hair ritually at the time of marriage. Artemis will bestow a crowning irony on Hippolytos at the end of the play when she

promises him, as he lies dying, a kind of perverse immortality
(1528–1536/1424–1429):

And to you, my poor catastrophe,
against such evils
I shall give the greatest honors in Trozen.
Unyoked girls before their marriage
will cut their hair for you.
For all time to come
you will reap the great grief of their tears.
Girls will make songs to tell your story
and Phaidra's love for you will not go unremembered.

Hippolytos' fame is eternally entrusted to girls on the brink of
sexual initiation and intertwined with Phaidra's passion. How
very odd for him.

Gods are big. Gods can enlarge us. Artemis' view of what's
good for Hippolytos is much bigger than his own; her view of
sexuality sees virtue in virginity and marriage both. Flesh and
change make sense to her as part of the workings of necessity, be-
yond human control. Hippolytos' utter ignorance of such things
is made clear in the first scene of the play when he closes his
prayer to Artemis with the words (119/88):

So may my finish-line match my start.

He is using a metaphor from horse racing and I suppose his in-
tention is to pray for a life of consistent purity from beginning to
end. But what beginning, what end? Whose life can end as it be-
gan, as if it were a thing apart from time, as if flesh did not
change? Who lives apart from time except the gods? Perhaps
Hippolytos thinks he is a god. If so, his end shows him he is not.

But since his end is engineered by Aphrodite, it does in a way match his start. We all begin in an act of Aphrodite.

"Aphrodite's breath is felt / on everything there is." (633–634/ 560–562). Aphrodite is the name for all that Hippolytos wants to edit out of his view of reality. But this goddess, who introduces the play, designs the action and is present in every choral ode, cannot be got rid of. She begins the play by saying:

Much among mortals I am. . . .

This is a literal version. It sounds lame. The Greek word for "much" (*polle*) is untranslatable, because it has come over into English as a prefix for any concept involving muchness—polyphony, polygamy, etc. "Much" is an ordinary word. "Poly-" is a prefix that can turn up anywhere. She is not claiming omnipotence but rather universal access. Access that cuts across certain lines of morality or moral sentiment we might prefer the gods to respect. What do Euripidean gods respect? Mainly their own prerogatives. How does this affect human beings? Always badly. What attitude does Euripides take to the matter? Hard to construe—something between resignation and satire. He seems to conceive it as his task to render the mentality and customs of each god as if he were a travel writer describing a foreign country. Each has its wines and weather, its masterpieces and tortures, its quaint notion of justice. All repay study but none is entirely predictable. "Gods should have more wisdom than men," says Hippolytos' servant in a peevish prayer to Aphrodite (152/119). But in fact she is just as wise as she needs to be. She knows how to get what she wants.

What of Phaidra? A tricky soul to capture, apparently; Euripides wrote two plays about her. This is the second. The first may have been called *Phaidra* or it may have been called *Hippolytos Veiled*. The Byzantine scholar Aristophanes tells us that the second play "corrects what was unseemly and worthy of rebuke" in the first. No one knows exactly what he means, as the first play doesn't exist except for nineteen short fragments and two line-paraphrases. People conjecture the first play may have depicted an aggressive and lascivious Phaidra, rather like Potiphar's wife in Genesis or Stheneboia in Greek legend, while the second tries to balance good and evil, moving Aphrodite into position as pivot of everybody's downfall. Pivot but not cause. Phaidra's victimization by the goddess of love has a domino effect on the other characters, as all are swept along in Aphrodite's revenge, yet each chooses and commits actions that collaborate with the divine plan and destroy another human. A large question of free will and determinism comes to mind. Euripides seems inclined to lead us into the middle of this question and leave us there. It makes me think of a hardboiled egg. Cut it open, you see an exquisite design—the yellow circle perfectly suspended within the white oval. The two shapes are disjunct and dissimilar yet construct one form. They do not contradict or cancel out, they interexist. Can you say one is prior? Circle as distorted oval? Oval as imperfect circle? Rather they each follow the other in a perfect system called egg.

Names, too, are a kind of system. We have already noted Hippolytos' prayer, "So may my finish-line match my start." Here is another way it comes true. His name means "loosed by horses." "Loosed" in the sense "unbound, unfastened, undone" and also "dissolved, destroyed, pulled apart" and also "opened, released, set free" and also "atoned for, paid off, made good." Aphrodite's justice requires that the man who refused the yoke of marriage should be dragged to death by the yoke of his own horses. Artemis' justice rewards Hippolytos for his pains by giving him a place in the wedding ritual, where brides are "loosed" from their virginity. You can see a kind of elegance in it, a kind of lesson. Yet you could also ask, Whose interest is served by attaching this lesson to Hippolytos from the day he was born, whose system is at stake and how could we ever grasp it?

There are days it is foggy in Venice. You cannot quite see the person you are following. But you can hear the feet going TAP TAP TAP away down the corridor. TAP TAP TAP there he goes ahead of you. TAP TAP TAP or is she behind you? TAP TAP TAP perhaps you are following yourself.

CAST OF CHARACTERS
In order of appearance

APHRODITE

HIPPOLYTOS, *son of Theseus*

(MALE) ATTENDANTS *of Hippolytos*

(MALE) SERVANT *of Hippolytos*

CHORUS

(FEMALE) NURSE *of Phaidra*

PHAIDRA, *wife of Theseus and stepmother of Hippolytos*

(FEMALE) SERVANTS *of Phaidra*

THESEUS, *king of Athens*

MESSENGER

ARTEMIS

The scene is set at Trozen, a city near Athens where Theseus is spending
one year of exile with his family. There are two side entrances and a
central building which represents Theseus' palace.

[enter Aphrodite from side entrance]

APHRODITE

You know who I am. You know my naked power.
I am called Aphrodite! here and in heaven.
All who dwell between the Black Sea and the Atlantic,
seeing the light of the sun—
all who bow to my power—I treat with respect.
But if they think proud thoughts at me
I bring them down.
The fact is
gods love to be honored by men.
Let me clarify that: 10
Theseus' child, born of a wild Amazon
taught by pure Pittheus,
Hippolytos,
of all the citizens of Trozen here
he alone
proclaims me the worst of divine beings.
He says *No* to sex and will not touch marriage.
It is Artemis, Apollo's sister, daughter of Zeus
whom he adores, holding her highest of all.
Through the green wood   20

he stays near her always,
near the virgin,
and with swift hounds
he scours animals from the ground.
He has fallen into a more than mortal friendship!
I don't envy it, why should I?
But for his crime against me
I will punish Hippolytos
on this day. The scene is set,
it won't be hard.   30
Once,
when he went from Pittheus' house
to view the sacred mystery rites,
his father's wife saw him—
highborn Phaidra.
That look seized hold of her heart:
desire is terrible. You see my plan.
Even before coming to Trozen
Phaidra had a temple built,
by the rock of Athene,   40
overlooking this land.
A temple to me.
(And in future people will call it
"temple of the goddess set over Hippolytos.")
For Phaidra burned with love for someone impossible.
But now
Theseus has left the land of Athens
fleeing bloodguilt
to sail here with his wife
for one year's exile.   50
And she groans.
She is pierced

with stings of desire, the poor one wastes away
and says no word.
None of the household knows her affliction.

But that's not how this love will end.

I intend to show it to Theseus, yes it will all come out.
And our young enemy will die
by his father's curse—
curses were given to Theseus once   60
as a prize
by Poseidon king of the sea:
three curses to pray and none in vain.

And Phaidra? She'll save her honor but die all the same,
Her suffering has no weight
against
my right to punish
enemies.
Here he comes.
He has left off hunting.   70
Hippolytos!
I'll go my way.
Big crowd with him, attendants behind,
shouting out honor for Artemis,
hymns for Artemis.
He does not know the gates of death are standing open.
This is the last daylight his eyes will ever see.

[exit Aphrodite by side entrance]

[enter Hippolytos with attendants from side entrance]

HIPPOLYTOS
  Follow,
    singing,
      follow   80
        the holy one of Zeus,
    Artemis,
    for whom we care.

HIPPOLYTOS AND ATTENDANTS
  Lady, lady of utmost reverence,
    child of Zeus,
      hail!
      I hail you O daughter
  of Zeus and Leto:
Artemis
    most beautiful by far of maidens,   90
    you who dwell
    in the great sky,
      in your father's courts,
        in the solid gold house of Zeus.
  I hail you O most beautiful most beautiful of those on
    Olympos!

HIPPOLYTOS
  For you
    this crown
      from a field uncut
  O queen I wove and bring—
  from a virgin field where no shepherd dares to graze his
    animal,   100
  no knife comes near it—
      field uncut,

just a bee dozing by in spring.
And Shame
   waters it with river dews.
No one can cut a flower there
except those who have
   purity absolute in their nature,
      untaught, all the time.
The bad are kept out.   ●   110
But O
   beloved queen
      for your golden hair
accept this crown from a reverent hand.
For I alone of mortals have the privilege:
with you I stay, with you I talk,
I hear your voice,
although I do not see you.
So may my finish-line match my start.

[enter (male) Servant from palace]

SERVANT
   You are my prince but gods are our masters, all.   120
   So will you accept some advice from me?

HIPPOLYTOS
   Yes. Or seem unwise.

SERVANT
   Do you know there is a law among men?

HIPPOLYTOS
   What law?

SERVANT

To hate high pride and bad manners.

HIPPOLYTOS

Of course, what proud man is not annoying?

SERVANT

And is there some charm in being courteous?

HIPPOLYTOS

Very much. And profit too.

SERVANT

And would you expect the same among gods?

HIPPOLYTOS

If mortals use gods' laws. 130

SERVANT

How is it then you refuse courtesy to a proud goddess?

HIPPOLYTOS

Which goddess? Be careful.

SERVANT

The goddess who stands at your gates, Aphrodite.

HIPPOLYTOS

From afar I greet that one, since I am pure.

SERVANT

Yet she is proud and important to men.

HIPPOLYTOS

No god adored at night is pleasing to me.

SERVANT

To honor gods, child, is an *obligation.*

HIPPOLYTOS

Different men like different gods.

SERVANT

I wish you good luck and good sense. You'll need them.

HIPPOLYTOS

Go, servants, into the house and to your supper.   140
Sweet after hunting is a full table.
My horses need a rubdown,
then after I've had my fill of food
I'll yoke them and give them a run.
You, Aphrodite,
keep out of my way!

[exit Hippolytos with attendants into palace]

SERVANT

We must not imitate the young in thoughts like these.
As becomes a slave, I shall bow
to your statue, Aphrodite be compassionate!
If someone who is stretched tight inside himself   150
talks reckless talk, best not to listen.
Gods should have more wisdom than men.

[exit Servant into palace]

[*enter chorus from both side entrances into orchestra*]

CHORUS (*entrance song*)
  Water from the river Okeanos drips
          down a certain rock
  (so it is said) and
  at its edge a stream
          where pitchers are dipped.
  There
  someone I know
  was soaking her redpurple robes   160
  in river dew,
          spreading them on flat rocks in the sun.
  From her to me
  first came the story of my lady

  wasting herself on a bed of pain:
          she hides her body
  in the house,
  covers her yellow hair.
  Three days
  (so I hear)   170
  she is without food,
  keeps her body
          pure of bread, longs to
  run herself aground
  in a sad secret death.

  Is it a god inside you, girl?
  Deranged by Pan, by Hekate?
  Or the holy mountain mother?

Or does Artemis, mistress of wild things,
devastate you?   180
For she ranges the lake
    and the sand
        near the sea and the wet salt places.

Or is it your husband, the king of Athens,
the highborn one—
is someone in your house coaxing him
to secret sex?
Or has some sailor out from Krete
brought to the queen
    harsh news   190
        that binds her soul to its bed with grief?

Woman has a wrongturned harmony:
    some evil sad helplessness
            comes to dwell in her
    when she has pain or despair.
That breeze shot through my womb once.
    But to Artemis of childbirth,
        the heavenly one
    who rules arrows,
I cried out   200
    and praise god!
    she came to me.

But here is the old Nurse at the door,
bringing Phaidra out of the house.
What is it—my soul longs to know—
what has so changed the body of my queen?

*[enter Nurse from palace with Phaidra on a bed
carried by (female) Servants]*

NURSE

Ah, humans and their ailments! Gas and gloom!
What should I do for you? Or not do?
Here is your daylight, here is your bright open air,
here is your sickbed brought out of the house—   210
"Outside!" you said. "Take me outside!"—
but any minute you'll rush back in.
Every joy disappoints.
What's here doesn't please you,
what's far off you crave.
Better to be sick than tend the sick.
The one is simple, the other
work, work, work, work and worry.
Now every mortal life has pain
and sweat is constant,   220
but if there is anything dearer than being alive
it's dark to me.
We humans seem disastrously in love with this thing
(whatever it is) that glitters on the earth—
we call it life. We know no other.
The underworld's a blank
and all the rest just fantasy.

PHAIDRA

Lift my body, raise my head.
I've gone loose in the joints of my limbs.
Take my hands, servants.   230
This headbinder is heavy,
take it away, let down my hair on my shoulders.

NURSE

There, child, don't throw yourself around so.
The disease will feel lighter
if you stay calm.
We all must suffer.

PHAIDRA

AIAI! [*cry of pain*] How I long for a dewcold spring
and pure running water!
To lie back
beneath black poplars,   240
to sink deep in the long grass of a field!

NURSE

Child, what are you shouting?
Don't say such things where people can hear.
Your words ride toward madness.

PHAIDRA

Send me to the mountains! I will go to the woods,
to the pine woods
where
hunting dogs race to the kill,
closing in on dappled deer.
How I long   250
to cry the hounds onward
and let fly a spear fly
from alongside my yellow hair,
floating
the weapon in my hand!

NURSE

Why harm yourself like this?
What do you care about hunting?
What do you want with cold running springs?
Right next to the wall is a stream where you can drink.

PHAIDRA

Queen of the salt lake,   260
Artemis,
lady of racetracks
where horses' hooves pound,
how I long to be on your ground
riding,
breaking
wild northern colts!

NURSE

Crazy talk!
One minute you're gone to the mountains to hunt,
the next you want colts and flat beaches!   270
It would take a mighty prophet to say
what god is pulling back the reins on you
and riding your mind off its track.
Oh child.

PHAIDRA

I am a sad one! What have I done?
Where have I gone from my own good mind?
I went mad, a god hurt me, I fell.
PHEU PHEU TLEMON! [*cry*]
Woman, hide my head again.
I am ashamed of my own words.   280

Hide me.
Tears fall
and my eye turns back for shame.
To think straight is agony.
But this madness is evil.
Best to die unaware.

NURSE

Yes I am covering you. But when
will death cover me?
Long life teaches many things.
Mortals must measure their love for one another,   290
not let it cut right through to the marrow of the soul.
Keep affections of the mind flexible, I say—
easy to let them go or pull them tight.
But when one soul feels the pain of two,
as mine for hers,
what a burden.
You know strict rules of life do more harm
than giving in to pleasure—
unhealthy, they say.
Excess is your culprit.   300
"Nothing too much," that's my advice.
And wise men agree with me.

CHORUS

Old woman, trusted Nurse of the queen,
we see Phaidra in a bad state
but no sign of the disease.
Please tell us, what is it?

NURSE

I don't know. She won't say.

CHORUS

What started it?

NURSE

Same answer. She is silent.

CHORUS

How weak and worn her body is.   310

NURSE

Well yes, three days without food.

CHORUS

Is she in a delusion or trying to die?

NURSE

Who knows? She doesn't eat, she dies.

CHORUS

Astonishing her husband approves.

NURSE

She hides her pain, won't say she is ill.

CHORUS

Does he not see the proof on her face?

NURSE

In fact he's away from home right now.

CHORUS

Then won't you use force, try to find out
what is making her sick, drifting her mind?

NURSE

I've tried everything! Got nowhere!   320
But I'm not giving up.
You can bear witness
what kind of woman I was for my mistress in trouble.
Come, dear child, let's both forget
what we said before: you be sweeter,
clear your brow, open your mind,
and I'll start again trying to reason with you.
Even if your illness is something unspeakable
there are women here who could help.
Or if it's decent for men to hear,   330
speak up! tell a doctor!
Silent now? What use is silence?
Correct me if I'm wrong
or agree if I'm right.
Say something! Look at me! Ah,
women, our effort is futile.
We are miles off.
She was not touched, she is not persuaded.
Well, know this—stubborn as the sea!—
if you die you betray your own children.   340
They will get no share of their father's house.
I swear by the horseriding Amazon queen
whose son is master of your sons—
that bastard who thinks he's the true son,
you know him well,
Hippolytos—

PHAIDRA

OIMOI! [*cry*]

NURSE

[*silence, waits*]

PHAIDRA

You destroy me, woman. By the gods
I beg you do not say his name again.

NURSE

You see? you are quite sane, yet unwilling   350
to help your children or save yourself.

PHAIDRA

I love my children. But I'm caught in the storm of a
    different fate.

NURSE

Your hands are clean of blood, child?

PHAIDRA

Hands are clean. The mind is filth.

NURSE

Is it bad magic, a spell cast by some enemy?

PHAIDRA

A loved one destroys me, although he doesn't mean to.

NURSE

Theseus has done you wrong?

PHAIDRA

Oh no—and may I never seem evil to him!

NURSE

Well what is this dread thing that pulls you toward death?

PHAIDRA

Leave me to my sins, they are not against you.   360

NURSE

No I will not give up on you.

PHAIDRA

What then—force me? cling to my hand?

NURSE

Your knees too, I will not let go.

PHAIDRA

Evil, you unlucky woman, evil is what you will find.

NURSE

What greater evil than watching you die?

PHAIDRA

To hear it will kill you. My honor is in this.

NURSE

And you hide it though I plead with you!

PHAIDRA

Out of what is shameful I am contriving something good.

NURSE

Won't you get more honor if you tell it?

PHAIDRA

Get back, by the gods, let go my right hand!   370

NURSE

No I will not. You must tell it.

PHAIDRA

Yes. I must. I will. I respect your suppliant hand.

NURSE

I am silent. It's your story now.

PHAIDRA

O my poor mother, what a love you fell into!

NURSE

You mean her lust for the bull?

PHAIDRA

O my sad sister, wife of Dionysos!

NURSE

Child, what's wrong? Why talk old family scandal?

PHAIDRA

And third—me. Oh I am a sad one. I am lost.

NURSE

You frighten me. Where is this going?

PHAIDRA

To where our sorrows began long ago.   380

NURSE

Maybe I don't want to hear.

PHAIDRA

PHEU! [*cry*]
If only you could say it for me!

NURSE

I am no prophet of the invisible.

PHAIDRA

What is this thing they call falling in love?

NURSE

Something absolutely sweet and absolutely bitter at the same time.

PHAIDRA

I feel only the second.

NURSE

You're in love? Child! Who is it?

PHAIDRA

That one, whoever he is, the Amazon's—

NURSE

Hippolytos?   390

PHAIDRA

You say it, not I.

NURSE

OIMOI! [*cry*]

What do you mean? Child, you destroy me.

Women, I cannot bear it, I will not endure it!

Hateful day, hateful light of day!

I'll throw myself—fall headlong—let my

life go! Farewell. I die!

The fact is there are people, good people who,

not because they want to

but all the same,   400

fall in love with the wrong thing.

Aphrodite is no god—

something bigger than a god if that exists—

who has ruined this woman and me and the house!

CHORUS

Did you hear O

did you listen O

to the queen cry aloud

her pain,

        her sad sorrow?

Dear lady, may I die before   410

I reach your state of mind.

        O poor lady in these pains.

        O sorrows that have mortals in their grip.

You are lost.

        You showed evils to the light.

What waits for you this day?

Something new and strange is beginning in the house.

Anyone can see
where the luck sent by Aphrodite will end,
    O you poor child of Krete.   420

PHAIDRA

Women of Trozen, you who dwell facing the Peloponnesos,
once in a while in the long night I ponder
mortal life and how it is ruined.
Not from bad judgment
do people go wrong—many are quite reasonable—
no look, it's this:
we know what is right, we understand it,
but we do not carry it out. Either from laziness,
or we value something else, some pleasure.
Pleasures are many,   430
long talks and idle time (that sweet badness)
and shame.
There are two kinds of shame.
One is harmless, the other kills a house.
If right action were ever clear,
these two things wouldn't have the same name.
So much for my views.
No love-charm can change them.
But I'll tell you the path my reasoning took.
When desire first wounded me I considered   440
how best to bear it. I began with
silence and secrecy—there's no trusting the tongue,
it loves to punish others
and draw disaster on itself.
Second, I tried to suppress my mad feelings.
That didn't work. You can't suppress Aphrodite.
So third,

my plan is to die.
An excellent plan, no one will deny.
If I do right there's no reason to hide it   450
but when I do wrong, I want no witnesses.
That my deed and my disease were dishonorable
I knew.
Realized too
that as a woman
I would be hated. I curse that one
who first shamed her bed with another man.
It began in highclass houses.
When corruption hits the rich
the poor soon join in.   460
I hate those women who talk self-control
but get hot inside.
Aphrodite! how can such a wife
look in her husband's face without fear—
what if the darkness, her accomplice,
what if the very rooms of her house began to speak?
For me, ladies, death is the answer.
I must not shame my husband
or children—I want them to live free,
in freedom of speech,   470
in glorious Athens, and to have a good name on their
    mother's side.
It enslaves a man, even a strong heart,
knowing his mother or father was evil.
To win at life
you need a good and righteous judgment.
Time holds up a glass to bad people
sooner or later,

as a mirror to a young girl.
Not me, I pray, not me.

CHORUS

   PHEU PHEU! [*cry*]   480
   Oh yes purity is a fine thing always
   and brings a good name.

NURSE

   Lady, your condition
   gave me a shock.
   But now I realize I was silly.
   Second thoughts are better, aren't they?
   It's nothing extraordinary, nothing inexplicable
   happening to you.
   A goddess's anger has struck you.
   You're in love? Is that surprising? You're not alone!   490
   And because of your love you want to end your life?
   Not much profit in desire then,
   if everyone touched by it has to die.
   Yes Aphrodite is unbearable in full flood:
   if you bend to her she comes on gently
   but if you act high and proud
   she will take you down, break you down, somehow.
   She moves through air,
   she exists in the ocean's
   rise and fall,   500
   Aphrodite!
   All things come to be from her.
   She is the sower and giver of desire,
   she is the reason every single person on earth was born!

Anyone
who reads old books or poetry
knows how Zeus once longed for sex with Semele,
how shining Eos ravished Kephalos for love.
Yet these dwell in heaven, they do not run away—
pleased, I think, to be mastered like this.   510
But you, you won't endure it?
Your father should have begot you on special terms,
with other gods for masters, if you won't accept these laws.
How many sensible husbands
pretend not to see a marriage bed defiled?
How many fathers procure
a bit of flesh for sinful sons?
That's human wisdom.
If you don't like the way it looks, close your eyes!
Perfection is not for mortals.   520
No use trying to fit the roofbeams of your house
dead straight!
It's deep trouble
you've fallen into—do you imagine
you'll just swim away?
You know, if a person has more good than evil
in a human life, he's doing all right.
Beloved child, stop this wrongheadedness,
stop being arrogant—this is nothing else than arrogance,
to want to be stronger than the supernatural.   530
Endure your passion. A god made it happen.
You are sick. Change that.
Spells and magic words exist.
Some cure will appear.
If men are slow
we women will find a way.

CHORUS

Her advice is helpful, Phaidra,
but it's you I praise.
Still, this praise may be painful to hear.

PHAIDRA

Here is something that ruins cities and houses of men—   540
words too beautifully said.
Words aren't for pleasure.
They should lead to a virtuous reputation.

NURSE

Oh stop moralizing. Words aren't the issue.
You need a man.
We have to get a grip on this,
tell it straight.
Your life is veering towards catastrophe, you're
out of control—you know I wouldn't have
led you on this far   550
just to serve your sexual pleasure.
But if life is at stake—and your life is at stake!—
no one can call it wrong.

PHAIDRA

You terrify me. Close your mouth!
No more obscenity, no more!

NURSE

Obscenity!—well maybe, but nice talk is useless.
Why not do the deed if doing it will save you?
You'll die in your pride!

PHAIDRA

No, for gods' sake! your words so seductive—
don't go further! My soul is all worked down   560
by desire—if you say these beautiful obscene things
I'll be caught! Lost!

NURSE

Fine, if that's what you want, stay sinless.
If not, do as I say. Call it a favor to me.
I have love-charms at home—I
suddenly remember—charms
for desire—not obscene, not harmful,
they'll stop this disease, unless you turn weak.
But we need some token from the man you desire,
from his hair or his clothes: something to bind you two
    as one.   570

PHAIDRA

These charms—ointment or potion?

NURSE

I'm not sure. Don't fret about details.

PHAIDRA

Your expertise scares me.

NURSE

Everything scares you. Why worry?

PHAIDRA

You'll tell Theseus' son.

NURSE

Relax. I'll do it right.
All I need is you, Aphrodite, queen of the sea:
work with me!
My other plans I'll tell to friends inside.

[exit Nurse into palace]

CHORUS (*first stasimon*)

Eros, Eros, deep down the eyes   580
you distill longing,
   sliding
sweet pleasure
     into the soul where you make war:
I pray you never come at me with evil,
     break my measure.
No weapon,
   not fire,
     not stars,
       has more power   590
       than Aphrodite's
   shot from the hands
of Eros, child of Zeus.

In vain, in vain, beside Apollo's river
and his shrine
   do Greeks
slaughter oxen.
     Yet that tyrant god who has the key
to Aphrodite's chambers of love,
       that god Eros   600

we do not worship,
 though he plunders
  mortal men
   and sends them
   through all
 manner of misfortune
when he comes.

Wild little horse of Oichalia
unbroken in bed,
 never yoked to a man,   610
never yoked to marriage,
  from her father's house,
like a running naiad,
  like a girl gone mad,
in blood,
 in smoke,
  in a wedding of murder,
   to Herakles
   Aphrodite yoked her,
 Aphrodite gave her,   620
 O
 bride of sorrow!

O holy wall of Thebes,
O river mouth of Dirke,
 you too could bear witness
how Aphrodite comes on.
  To flaming thunder
she gave Semele
  as a bride
and laid   630

the girl to bed
in bloody death.
Aphrodite's breath is felt
on everything there is.
Then like a bee
she
flicks away.

PHAIDRA [*standing near the palace door*]
Silence, women. I am destroyed!

CHORUS
Why? What's happening in the house?

PHAIDRA
Wait, let me hear the talk inside.   640

CHORUS
This is a bad beginning.

PHAIDRA
IO MOI AIAI! [*cry*]
Misery.
Oh my misery.

CHORUS
What are you saying, why are you crying out?
What fear sweeps over you?

PHAIDRA
I am lost. Come stand by the doors—
listen!—someone screaming in the house!

CHORUS

Tell me, tell me—
what evil has come?   650

PHAIDRA

Hippolytos is shouting,
abusing my servant.

CHORUS

I can't quite hear what he's saying,
can you?

PHAIDRA

Oh yes I can hear— "Arranging sex for your lady!" he
    cries—
"Corrupting the royal bed!"

CHORUS

OMOI! [*cry*]
You are betrayed, lady.
What can I do?
The secret is out, you are ruined.   660
AIAI E E! [*cry*]
Betrayed by a friend.

PHAIDRA

She has ruined me, exposed me,
with her helpful medicine.

CHORUS

What next? You're trapped.

PHAIDRA

Just one way out—quick death,
quick cure.

[Phaidra draws back out of sight but does not exit]

[enter Hippolytos and Nurse from palace]

HIPPOLYTOS

O mother earth! O open sunlight!
Such words are unbearable to hear.

NURSE

Silence, child,   670
before someone hears you.

HIPPOLYTOS

I can't be silent and listen to that.

NURSE

Please, by your right hand!

HIPPOLYTOS

Do not take my hand or touch my clothes.

NURSE

By your knees, don't—

HIPPOLYTOS

Don't what? You said your words were innocent!

NURSE

But not for everyone to hear.

HIPPOLYTOS

Surely a good story needs listeners.

NURSE

O child, don't break your oath.

HIPPOLYTOS

My tongue swore the oath. My mind is unsworn.   680

NURSE

Child, what will you do? Destroy those who love you?

HIPPOLYTOS

Love? I spit on that. Love is not corrupt.

NURSE

Be kind. It is natural for humans to make mistakes.

HIPPOLYTOS

O Zeus! Why have you settled on men this evil in daylight,
this counterfeit thing—woman?
If you wanted a human race
there was no need to get it from them:
men could pay down a sum of cash in your temple
and buy their offspring,
each according to his property value,   690
and dwell in houses free of females!
Is woman an evil? Yes! Clearly!
A father who begets and rears one

has to add on a dowry to get her out of the house.
And the man who accepts her has a flower of ruin.
Oh he'll delight in decorating
his bad little idol
with cosmetics and costumes,
poor fool! There goes the wealth of his house.
Life is easiest for the man who marries a nothing.   700
Granted she's useless, but simple.
A clever female is something I hate.
May I never let into my house
a woman with a mind.
Aphrodite plants more evil in the smart ones.
A dull woman avoids folly through sheer lack of wit.
And we ought not let servants attend them,
but house them with animals—
animals that bite but have no voice:
no one to gossip with, no one to answer.   710
For they sit indoors all day contriving evil
and the servants carry it outside.
So you—you degradation—you
come to me to traffic in my father's inviolable bed!
I shall wash you out of me with pure running water,
dash it into my ears.
How can I be a bad man
when even to hear such things makes me feel unclean?
Realize this, woman: my piety saves you.
Had I not been caught off guard by oaths to the gods   720
I would have told my father all.
Now I'm leaving the house, until Theseus returns.
And yes, I'll keep silence.
But I shall watch, with my father's coming,
how you meet his eyes, you and that lady of yours.

Curse you!
I shall never get my fill of hating women,
not though I repeat this till the end of time.
Their evil is eternal.
Let someone teach them purity   730
or I'll trample them underfoot forever.

[exit Hippolytos by side entrance]

PHAIDRA
Sad O
   disastrous
   the fates of women.
What tricks
   or language have I now
to loose the knot I've tied?
Justice arrives. O earth and daylight!
   Where can I escape my luck?
   How shall I hide my trouble, ladies?   740
What god
   or mortal man
would stand by me in unjust deeds?
For the pain that is on me
is moving across, all the way across, to the other side of life.
   Disaster!

CHORUS
PHEU PHEU! [*cry*]
The deed is done. Clever contrivances of your servant, lady,
have not turned out well. Things look bad.

PHAIDRA

O you agent of ruin! Corrupter of trust!   750
What have you done to me!
May Zeus
my forefather
grind you to nothing,
blast you in fire from the face of the earth!
Didn't I see this coming—did I not command you
to keep silent? And now my humiliation!
You would not hold back.
Because of you
I'll die in shame.   760
Oh I need all new plans!
That man bitten to the brains with anger as he is
will speak against me to his father—tell your crimes—
and fill the land with my disgrace.
Curse you!
Curse anyone eager
to help a friend to ruin!

NURSE

Go ahead and blame my failures, lady,
for the sting is stronger than your judgment now.
But I have answers too, if you allow.   770
I reared you, I am on your side.
I sought a cure
for your disease and found one not so nice.
Yet if I had succeeded you'd call me smart.
Smartness is relative to winning, isn't it.

PHAIDRA

So this is justice? This is supposed to be enough for me?
You cut me to the nerves and then say "Sorry!"

NURSE

We're wasting words. I went too far.
But, child, there is a way to save the situation even now.

PHAIDRA

No more advice.   780
It was bad before.
Go—look to your own affairs, I'll manage mine.

[exit Nurse into palace]

And you, noble women of Trozen,
grant me this favor I beg.
Keep in silence what you heard here.

CHORUS

I swear by reverend Artemis daughter of Zeus,
I'll show none of this to the light of day.

PHAIDRA

Ladies, thank you.
One last thing.
I've got an idea   790
how I can leave my children a respectable name
and allow myself a way out.
For I will not shame my Kretan home
nor come to Theseus charged with corruption,
just to save one life.

CHORUS

What do you intend?

PHAIDRA

To die. How I'm not sure.

CHORUS

Hush.

PHAIDRA

Hush nothing.
I will pleasure Aphrodite, the one who destroys me,   800
by releasing myself from life this very day.
Bitter the love by which I'm beaten.
But I shall become
disaster for another
as I die—may he learn
not to swell himself on my misfortune.
If he gets a share of this disease
he'll learn self-control.

[exit Phaidra into palace]

CHORUS (*second stasimon*)

I long for the secret sunwalked places,
    and a god to take me up high   810
        amid high birds flying,
to rise and soar
    over seacoasts
        and rivers
            where sad girls
            pitying Phaethon

drop into the deepblue wave
their amber tears, their brilliant tears.

To the applesown shore where Hesperides sing
    I would make my way,   820
        where the lord of dark water
lets no sailor go further
    for he sets a solemn limit
        at the edge of Atlas,
            and ambrosial springs flow
            past the bed of Zeus
    while holy earth blesses
the blessedness of gods.

O whitewinged ship of Krete
    that brought my queen   830
    over beating waves,
salt waves, to kiss
the lips of bad marriage:
    black omen
    black bird that flew
    from Crete to glorious Athens
where they made the ropes fast in the harbor
and stepped ashore.

Unholy desire—Aphrodite's
    dread disease—   840
    broke her mind.
Beating waves,
waves.
    Noose hanging.
    Hard knot.

White throat.
Shamed in her fate, but lifting her name clear,
she rids her mind at last of bitter desire.

NURSE [*from inside*]
   IOU IOU! [*cry*]
   Run! Help! All you in the house!   850
   Theseus' wife is hanged!

CHORUS
   PHEU PHEU! [*cry*]
   It is over!
   She swings in a rope.

NURSE
   Hurry! Someone bring a knife
   to cut the knot from her neck!

CHORUS
   Ladies, what should we do? Enter the house,
   loose the queen from strangling ropes?
   Why? Aren't there servants around?
   Not safe to meddle.   860

NURSE
   Lay her out, straighten the pitiful body.
   Here is bitter housewarming for the lord of the house.

CHORUS
   Poor woman is dead, so I hear.
   They are laying her out as a corpse.

[enter Theseus from side entrance]

THESEUS

Women, what in the world
is that shouting in the house?
That wailing.
It's odd they give me no welcome at the door
when I come from afar.
Has something happened to Pittheus?   870
He is old, yet his passing would grieve me.

CHORUS

It is not the old whose fate concerns you,
Theseus. Young deaths are your pain.

THESEUS

OIMOI! [cry]
Am I robbed of a child?

CHORUS

The children live—heartbreak for you—their mother is dead!

THESEUS

What are you saying? My wife dead? How?

CHORUS

Hanged herself in a noose.

THESEUS

Seized by despair? What despair? What happened?

CHORUS

That's as much as I know.   880
I've just arrived to the mourning.

THESEUS

AIAI! [cry]
Why did I crown my head with leaves of joy?
There is no joy.
Undo the bars, servants, open the doors,
so I can see the bitter sight
of my wife. In dying she kills me.

CHORUS

IO IO TALAINA MELEON KAKON! [cry]
Oh woman of sorrows:
you suffered, you worked   890
such work as may pull this house down.
AIAI! [cry]
You had the nerve
for violent death, unholy death,
gripping it in your own hand.
Who is it, TALAINA! sad one, who obliterates you?

THESEUS

OMOI EGO! [cry]
Pity me!—pity this pain,
O TALAS! [cry]
the worst evil of my life.   900
O luck,
how heavily you fell on me and on my house.
Stain of some old vengeance—who knows why?—
grinding my life to nothing.

I am staring at a sea of evil: O TALAS! [*cry*]
I cannot swim it! I can never cross it!
What do I say—what was it came on you,
crushed you, woman—what do I say?
You are like some bird gone from my hand,
leapt into hell.   910
AIAI AIAI! [*cry*]
These are deep sorrows, deep sad sorrows.
From far away, from who knows where, I am gathering up
a luck sent by gods, because of the sins of somebody long ago.

CHORUS

Evils like these are not yours alone.
Others have lost a good wife.

THESEUS

Darkness of hell, quiet darkness of hell,
how I long for it! Long to lie dead.
Robbed as I am of the world of your love.
Your death is my death.   920
Who will tell me
poor woman,
why ruin swept over your heart?
Can anyone tell me what happened—or does this
crowd of servants huddle useless in my house?
OMOI MOI SETHEN MELEOS! [*cry*]
What pain have I seen here,
not endurable, not sayable.
Death.
House empty. Children orphaned.   930
AIAI AIAI! [*cry*]
You left me, you left,

beloved one,
finest of women seen by the light of the sun,
or the starfaced night.

CHORUS
O TALAS! [cry]
How much evil your house holds!
I let fall tears for your fate.
But I tremble at pain to come.

THESEUS
EA EA! [cry]   940
Wait, what is this tablet in her dear hand?
What news does it have?
Has the poor woman written a letter to plead
for our marriage, our children?
Poor sad darling, do not fear. To Theseus' bed
and Theseus' house
no woman will find entry.
Here, the imprint of her ring,
how sweet to see.
Let me undo the threads of the seal   950
and see what this tablet will say.

CHORUS
PHEU PHEU! [cry]
God is adding evil to evil.
People die.
The master's house falls.

THESEUS
OIMOI! [cry]

Evil on evil!
Not endurable not sayable!
O TALAS EGO! [*cry*]

CHORUS
  Tell me.   960

THESEUS
  It shouts, this tablet shouts aloud. Unforgettable things.
  Where can I go to escape it?—weight of evils!
  What a song, what a song this tablet sings!

CHORUS
  AIAI! [*cry*]
  Bad beginning. What more?

THESEUS
  This is repulsive.
  Why hold back?
  IO! [*cry*] O city!
  Hippolytos has dared to touch my marriage bed—
  raped it! polluted the sacred eye of Zeus!   970
  Father Poseidon! you promised me
  three curses once.
  If those were real curses
  annihilate my son this day!

CHORUS
  King, pray this back, for gods' sake!
  Or you will know the wrong of it another day. Hear me.

THESEUS

No.

And in addition I banish him from the land.
One doom or another will strike him down:
either Poseidon will honor my curses   980
and send him dead to hell
or else he'll go off into exile
and spill his bitter life on strangers' ground.

CHORUS

Here comes your son this very moment:
Hippolytos.
King Theseus, give over anger
and think what is best for your house.

[enter Hippolytos]

HIPPOLYTOS

I heard your shout and came running, father.
Why did you shout?
EA! [*cry*]   990
What is this? Your wife dead!
How can it be? I just left her—
eyes wide open on the daylight.
What happened? How did she die?
Father, I want to know. Tell me.
You are silent?
Silence is no use in disaster.
Surely you shouldn't hide troubles
from your closest loved ones, father.

THESEUS

    O mankind so deluded! so pointlessly deluded!   1000
    Why investigate, study, devise ten thousand technologies
    yet you do not know this one thing and cannot grasp it:
    how to teach a mindless man to think.

HIPPOLYTOS

    That would be quite a genius
    who could make fools think.
    But this is no time for philosophy, father,
    I fear your sorrows make your tongue go wild.

THESEUS

    PHEU! [*cry*]
    What human beings need is some clear index
    of who is a friend and who is not—   1010
    a diagnostic of soul—
    and every man should have two voices,
    one righteous and the other however it happens to be,
    so that the righteous voice could refute the unrighteous
    and we would not be duped.

HIPPOLYTOS

    Has someone slandered me to you?
    But I've committed no crime!
    Your words fill me with dread,
    slipping, strange words.

THESEUS

    PHEU [*cry*] the human mind! To what lengths will it   1020
      not go?
    Where will its reckless impudence end?

For if it swells from life to life
and each one exceeds the one before in evildoing,
the gods will have to add another world to this one
to make room for the unjust and the bad.
Look at this man: my own son yet
he shames by bed! And stands denounced
by this dead woman
as plain and utter evil.
Show your face to your father, polluted as you are!   1030
Are you the one who walks with gods as if you were
    something special?
You, the model of purity, uncut by sin?
No—to credit your boasts
is to call the gods stupid.
Go ahead, exalt yourself, sell your story—
the vegetarian diet, the Orphic jargon,
all that Bacchic business and spooky writings!
You stand exposed. I tell the world:
avoid such men.
She is dead. You think that will save you?   1040
No, you are caught, you thing of evil.
What kind of oaths, what words
could exonerate you?
Will you say she hated you, that a bastard
is always the enemy of legitimate sons?
She made a bad bargain, the way you tell it,
destroying her own dear life just to discomfit you.
Or do you claim that lust isn't natural to men,
just women? I don't see
young men are any more controlled than females   1050
when Aphrodite mixes up their blood.
The fact of being male is good in itself but—

oh why do I bother to argue with you?
Isn't her corpse right here the clearest witness in the world?
Get yourself out of this land as fast as you can.
You are exiled!
Don't come near godbuilt Athens,
don't cross any frontier I rule!
If after suffering this I am bested by you,
I'll lose my reputation as a scourge of bad men,   1060
they'll say
no scoundrel ever felt my punishing hand.

CHORUS

Who can call any mortal happy?
Look how beginnings are turned upside down.

HIPPOLYTOS

Father, the passion and set of your mind are terrifying.
But the case you make, although elegant,
is wrong.
Now I boast no skill at public speaking
(I prefer to address a few of my peers,
and I guess this makes sense—   1070
if you think what kind of people impress a crowd!)
still, there is a necessity. I must
loose my tongue. I'll begin
from the first accusation you made,
which you presumed I could not answer.
You see this daylight, this earth?
Nowhere in it is there a man—
go ahead deny it!—more purehearted than I.
I know how to worship gods,
and I choose my friends from honorable people,   1080

people ashamed to connive at evil
or do dirty favors.
I am not a man to mock my companions, father,
I am the same to friends absent or present.
And there is one sin that has never touched me—that sin
in which you think me caught—
my body is pure of sex to this day.
I do not know the deed except from hearsay, pictures.
Nor do I want to.
I have a virgin soul.   1090
No doubt my chastity fails to persuade you—well,
explain then how I was seduced.
Was this woman's body more lovely than any other in the
   world?
Or did I
take the heiress to bed to get your house?
Then I was a fool—mad, really!
But men who crave royal power are scarcely sane, are they?
No, never, never in the world! those who find
power sweet have had their wits turned by it.
Sure I'd like to win at the Olympic Games   1100
but in politics second place is fine.
I am happy with men of virtue as my friends—
the kind of influence that brings no risk—
much more pleasant than tyranny.
Nothing left to say but this:
if I had a character witness here,
or if I were pleading my case with her alive,
the facts would show you who is evil.
But now I swear an oath to you
by Zeus who guards oaths,   1110
by the plain of earth,

I never touched your marriage bed.
I never wanted to.
I never took the thought in mind.
May I perish unknown and nameless,
may neither sea nor land receive my flesh when dead,
if I was an evil man.
What despair drove this woman to end her life
I don't know.
I can say no more.   1120
She was not pure but she did one pure thing.
Whereas I—my purity has ruined me.

CHORUS
Good. The oath was a nice touch.

THESEUS
Swindler! Sorcerer!—thinks
to rule my soul with his mild manners,
though he has put his own father to shame!

HIPPOLYTOS
I wonder at your manners too, father.
If you were my child and I your father
and I thought you'd touched my wife,
I'd murder you, not sentence you to exile.   1130

THESEUS
How like you to say that! But no,
you won't die so.
Quick death is too kind.
I want you outcast from your father's country
bleeding a bitter life away in alien places.

HIPPOLYTOS

OIMOI! [*cry*]
Is that your intention? You won't
wait for time to condemn me, just
throw me out?

THESEUS

Beyond the Black Sea and the boundary of Atlas if I could,   1140
I hate you so.

HIPPOLYTOS

Without any test of oath or pledge or oracle,
without trial, you'll cast me out?

THESEUS

This letter denounces you plainly. No need
for divination! Let the birds of omen
fly over my head—be gone!

HIPPOLYTOS

O gods! why not speak out—
I am being destroyed for honoring you!
No. He would never believe me.
I'd break my oath in vain.   1150

THESEUS

OIMOI! [*cry*]
Your piety will kill me!
Out of my land! Go!

HIPPOLYTOS

Where shall I turn? Whose house
can I enter, exiled on a charge like this?

THESEUS

Go to someone who wants his women defiled,
one cozy with evil.

HIPPOLYTOS

AIAI! [*cry*]
That goes to the heart. This is near tears,
if I seem evil and you think me so.   1160

THESEUS

The time for tears was before
you raped your father's wife.

HIPPOLYTOS

O house! if only you could speak for me,
bear witness!

THESEUS

Wise of you to turn to voiceless witnesses.
But your deed speaks aloud.

HIPPOLYTOS

PHEU! [*cry*]
I wish that I could stand apart, observe myself
and weep for my own suffering.

THESEUS

> You are much more adept at self-worship   1170
> than at piety toward parents.

HIPPOLYTOS

> O most miserable mother! O bitter birth!
> Pity anyone who is a bastard!

THESEUS

> Drag him out, servants!
> Do you not hear me pronounce him exiled?

HIPPOLYTOS

> No.
> You do it. You do it.

THESEUS

> I will if you don't obey.
> Your exile stirs no pity in me.

HIPPOLYTOS

> So, it is fixed.   1180
> Sad, what I know I cannot tell.
> O most adored of gods, Artemis,
> comrade, partner in the hunt, we shall go into exile
> from splendid Athens.
> Farewell city,
> farewell land of Erechtheus.
> O plain of Trozen,
> how many joys you gave to youth and time!
> Farewell.
> Looking at you, never again, I call your name.   1190

Hippolytos

Go, young men, companions,
say farewell and send me from this country.
Never will you see a purer man than me,
though my father holds otherwise.

[*exit Theseus and Hippolytos*]

CHORUS (*third stasimon*)
    The way gods care for us, when I think of it,
      lifts my pain,
        gives me secret hope,
          but then I look at the swings and swerves of mortal
            fate and I falter.
    Change rolls upon change. The life of man is a wandering
thing, pounded from all sides.   1200

I wish that I could say a prayer and have this fate from god:
    luck, wealth,
      a heart uncut by grief.
        Let my thinking be flexible but not false,
      and ride a happy life from day to day
on easymoving ways.

My mind is no longer clear. I see things paradoxical,
    see Athens' brightest star
      sent to another land
        by his father's rage.   1210
          O sands of the city's shore,
          O mountain oaklands where he ran his dogs
      and killed wild beasts
for holy Artemis.

Never again will he mount his mares and make the lake road
  drum with horses' feet.
    Music that never slept
      on the strings of his lyre
        will go silent through the house,
      haunts of Artemis will go uncrowned   1220
    in the deep green.
Brides' rivalry for your bed is ended.

In sadness for you
  I shall live a life of tears, a lifeless life.
    O poor mother,
      you had him for nothing.
        PHEU!
        I rage at the gods!
        IO IO!
        O you Graces who walk hand in hand,   1230
    why do you cast
  the blameless boy
out of his home?

I see a servant of Hippolytos
coming at a run, his face is dark.

MESSENGER
Where shall I find King Theseus, women?

CHORUS
Here he is from the house.

[enter Theseus]

227

MESSENGER

Theseus, I bring disturbing news
for you and the citizens of Athens and Trozen.

THESEUS

What is it? Has some new catastrophe   1240
seized our cities?

MESSENGER

Hippolytos is no more—or almost.
His eyes are still open but he is slipping away.

THESEUS

Who did it? Someone else whose
wife he raped?

MESSENGER

His own chariot killed him
and the curses out of your mouth.
Curses from your father the sea god,
sworn against your son.

THESEUS

O gods! O Poseidon! So you really are my father!   1250
You heard my prayer!
Tell me how did justice close
upon that criminal?

MESSENGER

We were down by the shore where the waves break,
combing our horses,
weeping, for

someone had come to announce
Hippolytos could not set foot on this land again.
You had banished him.
Then he came along the shore,   1260
telling the same tale, and walking
behind him a crowd of friends, young men.
At last his tears stopped. He said,
This is insane! But my father must be obeyed!
Harness my horses,
the city is no longer mine.
Then every man made haste.
Before you could say "ready" we had the team
standing at the master's side.
He took the reins in hand,   1270
put his feet in the straps
and held up his arms to the gods:
Zeus, may I die now if I am evil.
And let my father realize he has wronged me,
whether I die or live.
He lifted the goad and laid it on.
We servants followed close on his car,
straight down the Argos-Epidauros road.
And when we entered the desolate region,
where a headland on this side   1280
lies out to the Saronic Sea,
there came a noise from underground, like thunder of Zeus,
a deep rumble—you'd shiver to hear it.
The horses raised their heads, pricked their ears to heaven.
Raw fear was on us,
whence came that sound.
Looking to shore, where the breakers hit,
we saw a huge strange holy wave plant itself on the sky—

the shore of Skiron was blotted out!
the Isthmos and rock of Asklepios vanished.   1290
Then swelling and spattering foam and sea on every side
it went boiling towards shore where the chariot was.
At the height of the surge
it put forth a bull—wild weird thing!
And the whole place was filled with *voice*—
what a sound, made you shake!
We could not watch—
panic fell on the horses.
The master, who knows horses,
seized the reins,   1300
whipped them around himself and dragged as a sailor
drags back on his oar.
But they took the bit in their teeth and ran
wildly on, indifferent to his hand,
the reins, the car.
And if he drove
towards the soft ground,
the bull would appear in front to turn him back,
maddening the horses with fear.
And when they charged toward the rocks,   1310
it came up in silence
nudging close by the chariot rail,
until it tripped them and capsized the car
and threw the wheel against a rock.
Chaos then: wheel hubs
and axle pins jumping in air
and the poor driver bound and dragged
in the knot of the reins—
his dear head pounding on rock.
The flesh broke apart. He cried out horribly: 1320

Stand! You were fed at my mangers,
do not annihilate me! O curse of my father, killing curse!
Who will save me? I am a good man.
I was a good man.
We ran to help—but got left behind.
And he,
loosing himself from his reins I don't know how,
fell,
breathing a little.
The horses vanished and that thing, that bull,   1330
over the rocks I don't know where.
I am a slave of your house, king,
yet this I will never believe:
that your son is evil.
Not even if the whole species of womanhood hangs itself
    by the neck.
Not if someone turns the entire forest of Ida into written
    accusations.
No. I know he was good.

CHORUS

AIAI! [*cry*]
New disasters!
No letup!   1340

THESEUS

In my hatred of him
I was glad to hear this. Still,
I respect the gods and him. He is my son.
I feel neither pleasure nor pain.

CHORUS

What now? Bring him here, or what is your wish?
To my way of thinking you should not
treat him roughly. Your child has suffered.

THESEUS

Bring him. So I can set eyes on
the man who swore he did not touch my wife
and refute him with his own catastrophe.   1350

[exit Messenger]

CHORUS (*fourth stasimon*)
You drive before you,
    Aphrodite,
        the unbending minds of gods and men,
                and at your side,
                flashing his wings,
                quick on his wings,
                Eros
    nets them.
Over earth and over ocean,
    Eros   1360
    flying,
    gold-appearing,
    rushing on their mad hearts
    binds them—
        all nature:
    mountain creatures, sea creatures,
        whatever the earth nourishes,
            whatever the sun blazes down on,
                and also men.

Over all these,
Aphrodite,
you alone
hold perfect power.

[enter Artemis]

ARTEMIS
I call you, king of Athens,
listen!
I, Artemis, daughter of Leto, call.
Theseus, you miserable man, why do you rejoice in this?
You have murdered your son, you have broken holy law,
believing the lies of your wife.
Obvious ruin is what you have here.   1380
How is it you do not take your body down to hell
and disappear in shame,
or fly up on wings
to escape this grief?
Since you have no more
share of life among good men.

Hear, Theseus how your evils stand.
I will not smooth them out, and it will pain you.
But I came for this, to show that your
child's mind was just, so he dies honorably.   1390
And to show what gadfly drove your wife—or was it
a kind of nobleness in her?
For she was pierced
by that god I hate—hateful to any virgin—
pierced with longing for your son.
She tried to win against Aphrodite

by means of her own good mind
but lost to the tricks of her Nurse,
who told all to Hippolytos on oath.
And he,   1400
as was just,
resisted the words but still
he could not break his oath,
even when you wronged him.
He had a pious nature.
Phaidra feared disclosure,
wrote a letter full of lies and killed your son.
Lies. But you believed her.

THESEUS
  OIMOI! [*cry*]

ARTEMIS
  Does it pierce you, Theseus, this story?   1410
  Wait.
  What comes next will make you cry out more.
  You know those three curses you had from your father—
  you used one, you abominable man!
  against your own son. You could have cursed an enemy!
  But your father, the sea god, did what he had to do,
  what he had promised.
  And you stand condemned
  in his eyes and mine:
  you did not wait for oath or prophecy,   1420
  asked no questions, made no inquiry,
  no, you were in haste
  to curse and kill the child.

THESEUS

    Lady, I am destroyed.

ARTEMIS

    Your actions were terrible. Still,

    you can find forgiveness.

    It was Aphrodite wanted things this way,

    to deepen her heart.

    And it is a law among gods,

    not to get in the way of one another's passions.   1430

    We stand back.

    But let me tell you, except I feared Zeus,

    I would not have accepted this dishonor—

    to let him die.

    I loved him more than any mortal.

    As to your crime,

    ignorance acquits you.

    And your wife, by death, made questioning impossible.

    So now on you this crashing wave of evils.

    On me, pain.   1440

    Gods do not rejoice when pious men die.

    The bad ones we annihilate—

    children, house and all.

CHORUS

    Ah, here is the poor man,

    his young flesh, his fair head,

    disfigured. O grief of the house!

    A twofold sorrow has come down

    on these halls, sent by gods.

[enter Hippolytos]

HIPPOLYTOS

AIAI AIAI! [*cry*]

Wretched I, by an unjust father   1450

unjust oracles,

   am utterly abused outraged maltreated defiled.

    Lost am I in misery OIMOI MOI! [*cry*]

Pains shoot through my skull.

Spasms jump the brain.

Stop! Stop moving!

E E E E! [*cry*]

O deadly horses fed by my own hand!

You have destroyed me, you have murdered me.

Gently, servants, gently!   1460

You are touching broken flesh.

Who is that on my right?

Lift me lightly,

cursed as I am

by the errors of my father. Zeus, Zeus, do you see this?

Here am I a pious man, a godfearing man,

a man who surpassed all in purity,

I go to death. I see Hades before me.

My life is lost.

All for nothing   1470

I strove to be pious towards men.

AIAI AIAI! [*cry*]

Agony! agony comes on me!

Let me go—TALANA! [*cry*]

I pray for healing death to arrive.

Kill me! O kill me,

man of pain that I am. I long for a blade

to cut through my life,

to lay it to rest.

O curse of my father!   1480
Some bloodstained inborn evil
of our ancestors
is working itself out,
it does not hold back,
it comes upon me—why in the world?
Why me when I have no guilt!
IO MOI MOI why me!
What can I say?
How can I end this?
I pray Hades' nightblack necessity   1490
lay me to sleep.
I am disaster.

ARTEMIS

Poor boy, you are yoked to such bad fortune.
Your own noble mind has ruined you.

HIPPOLYTOS

O fragrance of god! Even amid evils
I breathe you and my whole body lightens!
She is here where I am, Artemis the god.

ARTEMIS

Poor boy, yes she is, your most beloved god.

HIPPOLYTOS

Do you see, lady, my sad state?

ARTEMIS

I see. But tears are forbidden my eyes.   1500

HIPPOLYTOS

You have no huntsman, no servant now.

ARTEMIS

None. But you die beloved by me.

HIPPOLYTOS

No driver of horses, no keeper of statues.

ARTEMIS

Aphrodite who stops at nothing devised this.

HIPPOLYTOS

OIMOI! [*cry*] I realize now the god who destroyed me.

ARTEMIS

She thought you dishonored her, hated your purity.

HIPPOLYTOS

Three of us she destroyed, I see.

ARTEMIS

Your father and you and his wife third.

HIPPOLYTOS

I cry out in pity on my father's bad fortune.

ARTEMIS

He was taken by the tricks of a god.   1510

HIPPOLYTOS

O you poor sad unlucky man, O father.

THESEUS

I am lost, child. No grace exists for me.

HIPPOLYTOS

I groan for you more than me—you did wrong.

THESEUS

I wish I were the dead one, not you, child.

HIPPOLYTOS

O bitter gifts of your father Poseidon.

THESEUS

How I wish they had never come into my mouth.

HIPPOLYTOS

You would have killed me anyway, you were so angry.

THESEUS

Yes I was deluded by gods.

HIPPOLYTOS

PHEU! [*cry*]

If only mortal men could lay a curse on divine beings!   1520

ARTEMIS

Hush, let it go. Not even in the blackness underground
shall Aphrodite go unavenged—
her angers assaulted your body
merely because you are good.
I shall punish anyone she loves
with my own hand, with these inevitable arrows.

And to you, my poor catastrophe,
against such evils
I shall give the greatest honors in Trozen.
Unyoked girls before their marriage   1530
will cut their hair for you.
For all time to come
you will reap the great grief of their tears.
Girls will make songs to tell your story
and Phaidra's love for you will not go unremembered.
Now you, O child of ancient Athens, take
your child in your arms and draw him close.
In innocence you killed him. Men cannot help
but do wrong when the gods arrange it.
And you, I urge you not to hate your father,   1540
Hippolytos.
You had a fate that ruined you.
Farewell.
Not lawful for me to look upon the dying
or defile my eye with their last breaths.
And I see you are near this.

[exit Artemis]

HIPPOLYTOS
Farewell. Go, blessed virgin.
Lightly you step away from our long companionship.
But since you ask it, I end the quarrel with my father.
For I've long obeyed your word.   1550
AIAI! here it comes. Here comes the dark.
Father, take and hold me. Set my limbs straight.

THESEUS

OIMOI! child, what are you doing to me in my misfortune?

HIPPOLYTOS

I am dying. I can see the gates of death.

THESEUS

Leaving my hand unholy?

HIPPOLYTOS

No, I free you from this murder.

THESEUS

What are you saying? You release me from bloodguilt?

HIPPOLYTOS

I call to witness Artemis, who kills with her bow.

THESEUS

Beloved, how noble you are to your father.

HIPPOLYTOS

Farewell, father. Farewell. Now out of my way.   1560

THESEUS

OIMOI! for your mind that was pious and good.

HIPPOLYTOS

Pray to have such legitimate sons.

THESEUS

Do not forsake me, child, hold on.

HIPPOLYTOS

    My holding on is done, father, I die.

    Cover my face with your robe now.

THESEUS

    O glorious Athens and boundaries of Pallas,

    what a man you have lost!

    In misery now,

    I shall remember your evils, Aphrodite,

    I shall remember!   1570

CHORUS

    A single grief has come on all citizens here,

    no one foresaw it.

    There will be the falling sound of many tears.

    In the lives

    of great men

    lives great sorrow.

ALKESTIS

PREFACE

In the sacrifice the sacrificer identifies with the animal receiving the blow. Thus he dies while seeing himself die, and even by his own will, at one with the sacrificial arm. But it's a comedy![1]

There is something of Hitchcock about the *Alkestis*, with its big sinister central house where life becomes so confused with death as to split the architecture in two. Hitchcock's *Shadow of a Doubt* features such a house as well as a household of people blind to each other's realities, blind to their own needs, and a killer at the heart of it all. In Euripides, as in Hitchcock, we know who the killer is from the beginning; suspense is created around the slow transaction of the crime, which is in both cases foiled. Then comes a facile conclusion that ties off the plot but leaves our emotions strangely tangled. Euripides won only second prize in 438 BC when he produced *Alkestis*. Hitchcock's film was judged "antisocial and obscure" by critics in 1943. Both works explore the psychological weirdness of ordinary people and everyday existence by jarring comic and tragic effects against one another as if they belonged to the same convention. In fact no one knows what convention *Alkestis* belongs to. It was performed fourth on its program in 438, that is, following three tragedies and taking the place of a satyr play. It is not a satyr play (no satyrs) but neither is it clearly a tragedy or a comedy. Definitions blur.

1. Georges Bataille, "Hegel, Death and Sacrifice," *The Bataille Reader*, edited by Fred Botting and Scott Wilson (Oxford University Press, 1997), p. 286.

Life and death blur. People spend the first 390 lines of *Alkestis* asking "Is she dead yet?" and, although we watch her drop dead onstage and be carried off for burial, she reenters at line 864/1006* apparently hearty. Admetos for his part makes free use of clichés of lament like "I might as well be dead!" or "I envy the dead!" or even "Take me with you!" as his wife exits to Hades. Since he himself has arranged for her to die in his place, these sentiments strike us as bizarre. Bizarre too is the conversation between Admetos and Herakles at lines 438–480/509–550 in which Admetos seeks to conceal from Herakles the fact of Alkestis' death by means of a series of untruths, half-truths and awful puns.

Herakles himself is a walking confusion. According to myth he is at once mortal and immortal, son of both Zeus and Amphitryon. Literature finds in him material for comedy as well as tragedy—on the one hand, an oversized, dimwitted, drunken brawler, on the other, an all-suffering savior of humankind. In *Alkestis* he plays both parts. He is also instrumental in splitting the space of the stage into two contradictory areas, doubling the sounds of the play into joy and grief at the same time: it is for Herakles' sake that Admetos partitions his house at 478–4/9/548–9, pulling a sliding door across to keep Alkestis' funeral separate from Herakles' carousing. This desecration breaks the play apart, breaks death open. Out steps life.

What does Alkestis' resurrection mean for the sacrificial contract that Admetos had negotiated with Death? This question is never addressed in the play. Mathematically Death is down one soul; common sense (what the Greeks call Necessity) tells us such a situation can't last. But Herakles seems a character able to override common sense. He releases Alkestis simply by choosing to do so. As if to say, within every death a life stands waiting to be set

*Please note that the first set of figures given refers to the line numbers of the present translation, the second to those of the Greek text.

free, should anyone have the nerve to do it. As if to say, try look-
ing deep into a house, a marriage, or an idea like Necessity and
you will see clear through to the other side. Death, like tragedy,
is a game with rules. Why not just break the rules?

Rules broken by Euripides in *Alkestis* include the rule of
closure. What are we to make of the ending? Can we be sure
the veiled woman is alive? that she is Alkestis? that she will live
happily ever after with her husband and children? Critics have
doubted all these. There is a kind of nuptial drama staged in the
finale scene—perhaps a parody of the ancient Greek wedding,
which centered upon an unveiling of the bride before the eyes of
her husband and some exchange of words between them—that
stalls oddly at its peak moment. Here the bride is unveiled to her
husband at 971/1121 (or so it seems to me; critics doubt this too)
but she will not be permitted to speak for three days due to her
death-polluted condition. An eerie silence carries her into the big
dark house of her unconventional husband.

I find I want to say less rather than more about *Alkestis*. Not
because there is less in this play but because the surface has a
speed and shine that evaporate with exegesis, like some of Hitch-
cock's plots. Or a trembling of laughter, terrible if it broke out.

CAST OF CHARACTERS
In order of appearance

APOLLO

DEATH

CHORUS *of old men of Pherai*

(FEMALE) SERVANT *of Alkestis*

ALKESTIS, *wife of Admetos*

ADMETOS, *king of Pherai*

(MALE) CHILD *of Alkestis and Admetos*

(FEMALE) CHILD *of Alkestis and Admetos (mute)*

HERAKLES

PHERES, *father of Admetos*

(MALE) SERVANT *of Admetos*

The scene is set in Pherai, a city of Thessaly. The stage has two side entrances and a central stage building with door, which is the palace of Admetos, king of Thessaly.

[enter Apollo from palace]

APOLLO

    O house of Admetos! Here I sat at a servant's table
    although I am a god.
    For when Zeus killed my son Asklepios—
    smashed his chest with a lightning bolt—
    I went berserk and slew his sons,
    the Kyklopes who forge fire.
    Then the father imposed a penalty.
    I had to serve this mortal man as a serf.
    So he made me his guest and I came here, herded his cattle,
    kept his house safe to the present day.   10
    And because he proved a pious man,
    this son of Pheres,
    I preserved him from death—
    I tricked the Fates.
    The goddesses agreed, you see, to let Admetos go
    if he sent another instead of himself to Hades.
    He canvassed all his kin and friends—father, mother, no one he
        found

except his wife
willing
to die for him and leave the light behind.   20
She is in the house now, lifted by others' hands.
Her soul is breaking free.
This is the day she will die.
And I to avoid pollution must leave the house I have come to
    love.
Oh look, here's Death at the gate!
Punctual as ever.
He's come for Alkestis.
This is the day.

[enter Death from side entrance]

DEATH
    A! A! [*cry of surprise*]
    You! What are you doing here, Apollo?   30
    Plan to rob the dead of their prerogatives again?
    Make your own rules and cancel mine?
    It wasn't enough you blocked Admetos' death—
    that was a sharp move—swindling the Fates!
    And now here you are ready to fight for this woman.
    You know her promise is given.
    She has to die or her husband won't go free.

APOLLO
    Relax, I'm not breaking any laws.

DEATH
    Why the bow, if you're breaking no law?

APOLLO

I always carry a bow, it's my trademark.   40

DEATH

And you always favor this house, despite the law.

APOLLO

It depresses me to see a friend in trouble.

DEATH

So you will rob me of a second corpse?

APOLLO

I didn't *rob you* of the first one—there was no violence.

DEATH

Then how is it he's above the earth, not underground?

APOLLO

You contracted for his wife instead—that's why you're here.

DEATH

And I *will* take her. Down. Down under the ground.

APOLLO

Take her, go. I know I can't persuade you.

DEATH

What, to kill an appointed victim? That's my function!

APOLLO

No, to grant a delay.   50

DEATH
Ah, that's your game.

APOLLO
Is there no way Alkestis could live to old age?

DEATH
There is no way. I deserve what I deserve.

APOLLO
She's just one soul—you'll have her in the end.

DEATH
More prestige if I get them when they're young.

APOLLO
But an old woman might receive a lavish funeral.

DEATH
Your ethics benefit the rich, Apollo.

APOLLO
How do you mean? You're too clever for me.

DEATH
I mean they could buy the privilege of dying old.

APOLLO
So you will not grant this grace?   60

DEATH
I will not. You know who I am.

APOLLO

Yes—one hostile to men and by the gods abominated.

DEATH

You can't have everything. You can't just break the law.

APOLLO

You're brutal but you will be stopped—
such a man is coming to the house of Admetos!
Sent by Eurystheus on a mission to wintry Thrace.
He'll stay as a guest here
and wrest the woman away from you by force.
You'll forfeit our gratitude,
lose her all the same and be hated by me.   70

[exit Apollo by side entrance]

DEATH

Talk, talk, talk.
Whatever you say, she's going with me.
I shall enter and begin the ceremony of the sword.
Whoever has their hair cut by this blade
is consecrated to the gods below.

[exit Death into palace]

[enter Chorus from both side entrances into orchestra]

CHORUS (*entrance song*)

What is this quiet?
Why has the house of Admetos gone silent?
    No friend is near

to say if we should mourn the death of our queen
or if she still lives and looks upon the daylight.   80
Alkestis—most noble of women,
most valuable of wives!

Does anyone hear groaning?
   Or hands striking in the house?
      Or a cry as if the thing were finished?
         No, nor any servant at the gates.
            Has the black wave struck?
               O savior Apollo, I pray you appear!
               If she were dead, they wouldn't be silent.
               If she were a corpse,   90
         they'd carry her out.
      Why are you so sure? I don't feel sure.
How could Admetos bury his wife with no mourners?

But I see no lustral water in front of the gates,
   no clippings of hair on the threshold,
      as is the custom when someone dies.
         No sound of women beating their hands.
            Yet surely this is the appointed day?
               What appointed day?
               For her to go under the ground?   100
            You touch my soul, you pain my mind.
         When good people die,
      good people grieve.
That is our custom.

But is there no voyage one could make,
   no oracle to ask—

in Lykia or the deserts of Ammon—to save her life?
  Sheer doom is drawing near!
No, there is no altar, no priest I can approach.

If only Apollo's son were still in the daylight,   110
  she might escape the shadowgates of hell.
    For Asklepios used to resurrect the dead
  until Zeus shot him down.
Now what hope is left?
        All is finished for the queen.
    Altars are full, blood is flowing,
but there is no cure.

Look here comes a servant out of the house
in tears. What shall I hear?
Is Alkestis still a living soul   120
or dead and gone—we need to know!

[enter (female) Servant from palace]

SERVANT

Possible to say she is both alive and dead.

CHORUS

How could someone die and keep on living?

SERVANT

She falters and her soul is breaking free.

CHORUS

O Admetos what a woman you are losing!

259

SERVANT

The master does not know this yet—until he suffers it.

CHORUS

No more hope to save her life?

SERVANT

The destined day closes its grip.

CHORUS

So the rituals are under way?

SERVANT

All the ornament is ready for her burial.   130

CHORUS

Let her know she dies glorious, incomparable,
best of wives under the sun.

SERVANT

Who could deny it?
Who can surpass her?
How could someone more perfectly privilege a husband
than by dying in his place?
Of course the whole city knows this.
But you will be amazed to hear what happened in the house,
when she realized it was the appointed day.
She washed her white skin in river water,   140
took out garments from the cedar closet
and dressed herself beautifully.
Then she stood before the hearth and prayed:

"Lady, I go beneath the ground.
One last time I kneel to you and make entreaty.
Protect my orphaned children! Yoke the boy
to a loving wife and the girl to a noble husband.
Do not let them die like me untimely young,
but live out the full delight of life in the land of their fathers!"
Then she went to all the altars of Admetos' house   150
and wreathed them and prayed,
tearing off branches of myrtle.
She did not weep. She did not groan.
Her beautiful face showed no change.
But she entered her chamber,
fell on the bed and tears came.
She spoke:
"O my bed, here I loosed my maidenhood beneath a man,
for whom I die—farewell!
I do not hate you. You bring me to death   160
but I could not betray him.
Some other woman will own you now,
not better than me but luckier."
Then she kissed the bed, falling forward
and wet it all with her tears.
And when she had enough weeping, she pulled herself up
and went to go from the room,
but turned back, and went and turned back many times,
then threw herself again on the bed.
The children came weeping around her,   170
twining themselves in her robes.
She held them, kissed them, said goodbye.
All the servants were weeping throughout the house.
She gave her right hand to each, none was unworthy.

Such are the sufferings in the house of Admetos.
Dying would end them.
But alive, he has this bitterness he will never forget.

CHORUS
No doubt he grieves.

SERVANT
He wails and clasps his wife in his arms,
begs her not to betray him, looks for a way out.   180
For she is wasting away, she is slipping away,
poor weight from his hands.
Nonetheless, barely breathing,
she still wants to look on the light of the sun
now for the last time.
I will go in and say you are here.
Not everyone has been loyal to this family in its troubles,
as you have.

[exit Servant into palace]

CHORUS (*first choral ode*)
O Zeus, what way out of evils, what loosing of fate could
there be?
AIAI! [*cry of sorrow*] Should I cut my hair   190
and put on black garments?
It is clear, all too clear, yet we pray to the gods.
Their power is absolute.
O Apollo, king of healing,
find some strategy for Admetos' pain.
Help us, help us! You did so before.

Come and release him from death.
Stop murderous Hades.

PAPAI! [*cry of sorrow*] O Admetos, what suffering is yours,
    deprived of your wife.   200
    AIAI! [*cry*] A man might cut his throat or hang himself.
        This day you will see your best-loved wife
            go down to death.
            Look, look, she comes, he is leading her out.
            Cry aloud!
        Lament, land of Admetos,
    the noblest of wives is fading away
underground to Hades.

Marriage, I think, is no glad state,
to judge from the past as well as this poor king.   210
Once he loses his woman
he'll live something not quite a life.

[enter Alkestis from palace with Admetos, two children, some servants]

ALKESTIS
    O Helios! O light of day!
    O racing clouds and motions of heaven!

ADMETOS
    They look, they see us suffering.
    We did no harm to gods and yet you die.

ALKESTIS
    My house! My home!
    My bridal bed! My father's land!

ADMETOS

    Lift yourself, O my dear, do not betray.

    Beg the gods to pity us.   220

ALKESTIS

    I see the black boat on the black lake.

    I see the old man who ferries corpses across,

    hand on the rudder,

    Charon is calling my name.

    Why do you linger? Time to leave. Hurry Alkestis!

    Charon calls.

ADMETOS

    Bitter crossing. OIMOI! [*cry*] Poor lady, what pain is ours.

ALKESTIS

    He is pulling, pulling—don't you see?—pulling me away

    to the place where the dead gather.

    I see his blue eyebrows, black wings beating—Death!   230

    Let me go, Admetos, what are you doing? Let go.

    The dark road opens before me.

ADMETOS

    Pity your loved ones! Pity most of all me!

    This grief we share.

ALKESTIS

    Let me go, lay me down, my feet falter.

    Hades is near.

    Night and shadows steal over my eyes.

    Children, your mother

no longer is.
Farewell, little ones, in the light.   240

ADMETOS

OIMOI! [*cry*] Your word is pain.
Greater than any death.
Do not, I pray you, betray me!
Do not orphan your children—
rise! Fight!
Your dying is my dying.
In you I exist—to live or not.
And I worship your love.

ALKESTIS

Admetos, you see my condition.
Now listen to my dying wish.   250
Because I prize you more than my own living soul,
I die—I did not have to die—for you.
I could have married some other man of Thessaly,
I could have dwelt in a princely house.
I did not want to stay alive without you, Admetos,
without a father for my children,
although I was young and I loved being young.
Your parents betrayed you.
It would have been a beautiful gesture, a noble gesture,
for them to save your life.   260
And you were their only son, no hope of more.
So you and I could have lived our remaining lives.
You would not be left alone to mourn me
and see your children motherless.
Well, some god worked things out this way.

So be it.
But you—*remember what you owe me.*
I have a request.
It is just, as you will agree.
For you love these children no less than I.   270
Do not put a stepmother over them.
Let them be masters in this house,
not persecuted by some jealous second wife.
No—I beg you.
For a new wife hates the first children—
no gentler than a snake.
And a male child has a great tower in a father,
but you, my little girl,
how will your girlhood be with another mother?
What if she slanders you and ruins your chance of marriage?   280
For I will never adorn you as a bride
or encourage you in childbirth, dear one,
where a mother's presence is a great solace.
I must die
not tomorrow, not the third day of the month, but now.
Farewell and stay happy.
You, husband, say you had the best of wives.
And, O my children, that you had the best mother.

CHORUS

I can't speak for him.
Surely he will do these things.   290

ADMETOS

I will do these things. No fear.
You were called my wife when alive and will be so after death.
No bride will ever take your place—

no one of such beauty or nobility exists.
My children are enough. I pray the gods allow me
to have my joy of them. For I did not have my joy of *you*.
I will mourn you not for a year
but my whole life, dear woman,
loathing the mother who bore me and my enemy father.
Their love was made of words not deeds.   300
But you gave up your most valued possession
to save my life.
Should I not groan aloud at the loss of you?
I will put a stop to revels and drinking and garlands and
    music—
they used to fill my house!
I'll never touch a lyre again
or raise my voice to the sound of the flute.
You take all joy of life away.
I shall have a craftsman
make a likeness of your body   310
and lay it in our bed.
There I can kiss it, hold it, calling your name
and pretend I have my dear wife in my arms.
A cold joy, to be sure, but what else is left?
Could you visit me in dreams? That would cheer me.
Sweet to see friends in the night, however short the time.
If I had Orpheus' tongue
if I could charm Persephone and win you back from Hades,
I'd go down there.
The dog of hell wouldn't stop me.   320
Charon wouldn't stop me.
I'd recover you to light!
But no. Wait for me there. Make ready our house.
When I die, we'll be together again.

For I'll have myself placed in the same cedar box as you.
My body next to your body.
Never separate again.
You alone were faithful to me.

CHORUS
And I, as friend for friend,
will bear this grief with you.   330

ALKESTIS
Children, hear this!
Your father vows he will not set another wife over you,
not take from me my honor, ever.

ADMETOS
Yes I vow it. And I will keep this vow.

ALKESTIS
On such terms receive the children from my hand.

ADMETOS
I receive them, gift of love from a hand of love.

ALKESTIS
Become now their mother in place of me.

ADMETOS
I must do so. They are robbed of you.

ALKESTIS
O children, though I should be alive, I go below.

ADMETOS

OIMOI! [*cry*] What shall I do without you? 340

ALKESTIS

Time will soften this. The dead are nothing.

ADMETOS

Take me with you, for gods' sake, take me below.

ALKESTIS

Aren't there enough people dying for you.

ADMETOS

O my fate! What a wife you are tearing from me!

ALKESTIS

Here it comes, the heavy dark upon my eyes.

ADMETOS

I am destroyed if you leave me, woman!

ALKESTIS

You are addressing one who is no more.

ADMETOS

No, lift your head, don't abandon your children.

ALKESTIS

Not willingly! But I say farewell.

ADMETOS

Look at them, look! 350

ALKESTIS

Farewell.

ADMETOS

I am destroyed.

[Alkestis dies]

CHORUS

She is gone. The wife of Admetos lives no more.

CHILD

IO MOI TYCHAS! [*cry*] She is gone! my mother is gone
out of the sunlight forever.
She left my life stranded, I am alone.
Look at me, look at my eyes, at my hands reaching out!
Hear me, O mother, hear me entreat you!
I call to you, I touch your lips,
I am your own little bird.   360

ADMETOS

She does not hear or see.
You and I are lost.

CHILD

Now I go my way alone.
She has left us!
O sister, how can we bear this?
Father, your marriage is empty.
She did not reach old age with you.
She is extinguished. And our house with her.

CHORUS

Admetos, have courage.

You're not the first nor the last man to lose his wife.   370

We all owe a debt to death, you know.

ADMETOS

I do know. And this evil did not drop on me suddenly—

I've been in pain for a long time.

But now, the funeral.

Abide with me, dear friends, and raise a paean

to the pitiless gods underground.

And to all in Thessaly I proclaim

mourning for this woman:

put on black garments, cut your hair, cut the manes of your
    horses.

Let there be no sound of flute or lyre through the town for

    twelve full months.   380

For I shall never bury one who means more to me than this.

She was the best.

She died for me alone.

[exit Admetos and children with Alkestis]

CHORUS (*second choral ode*)

O daughter of Pelias,

    farewell as you go into Hades,

        as you enter the sunless house.

            Let him know, the blackhaired god of hell,

        let him know, the deathconductor who sits at his oar,

    this is the best woman who ever crossed the lake of Acheron.

Singers will sing you, 390
 to the seven strings of the lyre,
  they will glorify you in songs without lyres,
   at Sparta when Apollo's sacred month comes round,
  in shining Athens when the moon sails all night long—
your death will make them sing.

How I wish I could pull you up to the light!
 Back from Hades' house and the river of hell.
  You alone, beloved lady, dared to change your husband's
   death
  for your own life.
  May the earth lie on you lightly. 400
 If he chooses a new bride
she will be a thing of hatred to your children and to me.

His mother said no, his father said no,
 they begrudged their own son.
  Old cowards!
  But you sent your young heart ahead of you
  to face death.
 If I found a wife like you—
rare thing!—she would be my lifelong joy.

[enter Herakles from side entrance]

HERAKLES
 Strangers! 410
 Is Admetos in the house?

CHORUS

He is, Herakles.
But tell me what business sends you to Thessaly.

HERAKLES

I have a labor to accomplish for Eurystheus.

CHORUS

Where are you headed?

HERAKLES

To capture the horses of Diomedes in Thrace.

CHORUS

How in the world? Are you not aware of how he treats his guests?

HERAKLES

No. I've never been to Thrace before.

CHORUS

You can't master his horses without a battle.

HERAKLES

But neither can I refuse a labor.   420

CHORUS

Well, you may come back, you may not.

HERAKLES

It won't be the first such risk I've run.

CHORUS

But why go after this?

HERAKLES

I must bring the horses back to Eurystheus.

CHORUS

Not easy to put a bridle on those jaws.

HERAKLES

Do they breathe fire?

CHORUS

No, they eat people.

HERAKLES

That sounds like wild mountain beasts, not horses.

CHORUS

You will see their stalls encrusted with blood.

HERAKLES

Who bred them?   430

CHORUS

Ares' son, or so he claims, the king of Thrace.

HERAKLES

Ares' son? That's my lifestory!
Uphill all the way.
I've had to fight the sons of Ares every one—

first Lykaon, then Kyknos, now this cannibal horsebreeder.
But no man will ever see Herakles turn and run.

CHORUS

Here's Admetos himself come out of the house.

[enter Admetos from palace]

ADMETOS

Herakles, son of Zeus! Grandson of Perseus! I welcome you!

HERAKLES

Admetos, king of Thessaly, good day to you too.

ADMETOS

Not so good for me in fact. But I know you mean well.   440

HERAKLES

Why do you look as if you're in mourning?

ADMETOS

I am to bury someone today.

HERAKLES

May gods keep your children from harm!

ADMETOS

My children are alive and well in the house.

HERAKLES

Your father then? At least he had a good long life.

ADMETOS

No, that one lives, as does my mother.

HERAKLES

Tell me it isn't Alkestis who's gone!

ADMETOS

Well, yes and no.

HERAKLES

What do you mean, yes and no?

ADMETOS

Both alive and dead—how the pain goes through me!   450

HERAKLES

I'm lost. You talk riddles.

ADMETOS

You know that she was doomed to die?

HERAKLES

Of course, she vowed to take your place.

ADMETOS

How can she really *live*, once that vow is made?

HERAKLES

A! [*cry*] Don't weep your wife before her time—you're way
ahead of yourself.

ADMETOS

She's as good as dead every minute—that's not being alive!

HERAKLES

Being and not-being are very different things, most people
think.

ADMETOS

Well, you have your view and I have mine.

HERAKLES

So why are you mourning? Who is it who's died?

ADMETOS

A woman. It was a woman.   460

HERAKLES

Your kin?

ADMETOS

Not kin, but still, absolutely necessary to us.

HERAKLES

How did she come to die in your house?

ADMETOS

She was orphaned and came to live here.

HERAKLES

PHEU! [*cry*]
How I wish I had not found you grieving.

ADMETOS

What are you suggesting?

HERAKLES

I'll go to someone else's house.

ADMETOS

Impossible, dear man. I wouldn't consider it.

HERAKLES

A guest is a burden when people are grieving.   470

ADMETOS

The dead are dead. Please come into my house.

HERAKLES

It's not right to have guests mixed up with a funeral.

ADMETOS

But the guest rooms are quite separate.

HERAKLES

Please let me depart. I'll be infinitely grateful.

ADMETOS

No, and that's that. Herakles will not go to another house.
[*to Servant*] You—go open the guest rooms on the other side of the house
    side of the house
and show him the way.
Make sure they shut the doors inbetween.
A guest at his dinner
shouldn't have to listen to groanings and grief.   480

[exit Herakles with Servant by side entrance]

CHORUS

    Admetos, what are you doing?
    In such extremity, you want to entertain? Are you mad?

ADMETOS

    Would you like it better if I drove my guest away?
    I'd look like I don't know the rules of civility!
    It would just add another layer of pain,
    to have my house called inhospitable.
    This man treats me superbly
    whenever I am his guest in thirsty Argos.

CHORUS

    But how could you hide your present sorrow,
    if this man, as you say, loves you?   490

ADMETOS

    He would not have been willing to enter the house
    if he knew my grief.
    Yes, maybe I'm crazy.
    But my house knows not how to dishonor guests.

[exit Admetos into palace]

CHORUS (*third choral ode*)

        O house of hospitality, generous and free!
        Apollo condescended to dwell here
    and shepherd your flocks on the slanting hills.
          piping them home.

He piped the spotted lynxes out from cover
and the lions down from their deep glens,   500
he danced the little deer
out of the dark of the pines.

And therefore, Admetos, your house is a treasure
beside the beautiful waters of lake Boibias.
Westward your plains stretch to the horizon.
Eastward all the way to the Aegean Sea
is yours to rule.

Even now, even in tears, you open your house to a guest,
though your wife is lying inside.
Noble impulse! I stand in awe. A good man   510
knows what he's doing.
Or so I trust.

[enter Admetos from palace with dead Alkestis, servants]

ADMETOS

Gentlemen, your presence is a consolation.
But now the bearers are bringing out the corpse.
You may greet her in the customary way
as she goes her last road.

CHORUS

But look, I see your father coming, with servants.
They have offerings for your wife, death offerings.

[enter Pheres from side entrance]

PHERES

> I come to help you bear your evils, child.
> For she was a good woman, a pure woman you lost—
>> no one will deny it. 520
> Bear up! Necessity is hard.
> But accept these offerings for the world below.
> Her body must be honored,
> since she gave her soul for you
> and saved me from a childless bleak old age.
> She has made her life more glorious than any woman's
> by this genuinely noble act.
> O lady savior! you raised us up when we were lost!
> Hail and farewell. May you be at peace in Hades' house.
> A marriage like this is worth having! 530

ADMETOS

> Who invited you?
> I don't count you a friend.
> And your offerings will never touch her, she does not need them.
> You should have done your commiserating then when I was in
>> trouble.
> But no, you stood aloof, you let another do the dying—
> though she was young and you are old—
> and *now* you want to mourn her?
> Are you supposed to be my father?
> Did *she* tell you that, my so-called mother?
> I'm not some slave's child smuggled in to her breast? 540
> Well, you've shown what kind of man you are.
> I do not call myself your son.
> Your cowardice stinks.
> You're old, your life is over,
> yet you wouldn't die for your own son.

You let this woman do it—not even born of our blood.
She is my mother and father now.
But you know, it would have been a beautiful prize to win—
dying for your son.
You've not much time left anyway.   550
And surely you've had all the blessings a man could want—
royal power, a son to succeed you,
not a childless house for others to usurp.
And you can't say I neglected you, that's no excuse.
I showed you all possible respect.
Such was my reward.
Well, hurry up and breed some more offspring, old man,
to care for your old age and put you in the ground.
I won't lift a hand!
I'm dead to you.   560
If I found another savior, if I look upon this daylight,
it's *her* I owe. It's her I should care for.
Old people are always complaining old age is hard and life
    too long.
But as soon as death shows up
you think again, don't you!

CHORUS
Stop. There is sorrow enough—why goad your father on?

PHERES
Who do you think you're talking to?
Some Lydian servant, some Phrygian slave?
I'm good Thessalian born and bred!
And you're shooting off your mouth like an adolescent.   570
You think you can just denounce me and walk away?
I gave you birth, I reared you up as master of this house.

I did not contract to die for you.
Whose law is it—that fathers die for sons?
It isn't Greek.
Your fortune good or bad is up to you.
I gave you all I should—dominion over stretching fields,
what I got from my father.
How did I wrong you? Where did I cheat you?
Don't bother dying on my behalf and I won't die on yours!   580
You enjoy life—don't you think I do?
I reckon we all get quite enough time underground.
Life on earth is brief but oh so sweet.
And you—talk about shameless!
You're only alive now because you sidestepped your own fate,
murdered your wife!
Yet you call *me* a coward?
Gallant fellow! A woman outdid you!
But you're not stupid, I admit—in fact you'll be immortal
if you keep on finding women to die for you this way.   590
So don't go badmouthing me, you cringing failure.
You love your life. So do we all—if that bothers you,
eat it.

CHORUS
    More bad words. Old man, stop.

ADMETOS
    Let him talk, I had my say.
    The truth hurts, doesn't it, when you're in the wrong?

PHERES
    Wrong? It would have been wrong to die in your place.

ADMETOS

A young man's death, an old man's death, same thing?

PHERES

We each get one life to live, not two.

ADMETOS

May your one life last longer than Zeus'.   600

PHERES

You curse your own father?

ADMETOS

I curse your greed for life.

PHERES

But aren't you burying this corpse to save yourself?

ADMETOS

Proof of your cowardice.

PHERES

I didn't kill her. You can't say that.

ADMETOS

PHEU! [*cry of rage*]
Some day I pray you'll have need of me!

PHERES

Just keep on marrying—get *them* to die.

ADMETOS

You are a disgrace.

PHERES

I love this light of God, I do.   610

ADMETOS

Your nature is base, you are not a man.

PHERES

I'm not *your* man.

ADMETOS

You will be infamous after your death.

PHERES

If I'm dead I won't care.

ADMETOS ·

PHEU PHEU! [*cry*]
You are a scandal!

PHERES

She's no scandal, though, is she?—just stupid.

ADMETOS

Go away and let me bury my dead.

PHERES

I go. You are about to bury your own murder victim.

And you will give justice for that: I bet   620
her kinsmen show up demanding blood.

[exit Pheres by side entrance]

ADMETOS

Go and be damned to you, you and that woman you live with.
Childless, as you deserve, go on with your endless old age.
You'll not enter this house again.
If I could disown you publicly I would.
[*to servants*] Let's go.
We must place this corpse upon the pyre.

[exit Admetos by side entrance with dead Alkestis, servants]

CHORUS

O she was brave!
     Poor brave splendid woman, farewell!
          May Hermes be kind,   630
     may Hades receive you.
     And if the good are recognized at all down there,
may the king of hell place you in honor by his side.

[enter (male) Servant from palace]

SERVANT

Many a guest has come to the house of Admetos,
every sort of person from every sort of place.
I've served them all.
But never
one so bad
as this.

He sees my master in mourning   640
and sails right on into the house anyway.
He realizes we are in disarray
but does he modestly accept what we have on hand?
No, he launches into a list of demands!
Then picks up a big ivy drinking cup in both hands,
drinks until the fire of wine is racing around in him,
crowns his own head with myrtle
and leans back to bay like a dog.
You could hear these two songs in our house at the same time:
him, on the one side, without a care for Admetos' pain,   650
us, on the other, bewailing our lady.
But we did not let the stranger see a tear.
Admetos forbade it.
So now I have to keep him entertained—
this gangster, lunatic, whatever he is—
while my lady goes from the house.
And I could not attend her!
Could not even stretch out my hand.
She was as a mother to me, to us all.
She knew how to soften the master's mood   660
and saved our skins many a time.
Guest or no guest, how I despise this trespasser on our grief!

[enter Herakles from side entrance]

HERAKLES

You there—why so glum? You're always frowning.
It's not good for servants to scowl at guests,
you should greet with a smile!
I'm your master's old friend, after all. Don't look so depressed—
she was an outsider wasn't she, not one of Admetos' kin?

Come here, let me share a bit of wisdom with you.
Have you given much thought to our mortal condition?
Probably not. Why would you? Well, listen.   670
All mortals owe a debt to death.
There's no one alive
who can say if he will be tomorrow.
Our fate moves invisibly! A mystery.
No one can teach it, no one can grasp it.
Accept this! Cheer up! Have a drink!
But don't forget Aphrodite—that's *one sweet goddess.*
You can let the rest go. Am I making sense?
I think so. How about a drink.
Put on a garland. I'm sure   680
the happy splash of wine will cure your mood.
We're all mortal you know. Think mortal.
Because my theory is, there's no such thing as life,
it's just catastrophe.

SERVANT

That I do know.
But I can't celebrate it with drink and laughter.

HERAKLES

Just because some woman is dead?
Don't take her so hard. The family is alive and well.

SERVANT

Alive and well? Don't you know what's happened?

HERAKLES

Of course I do. Unless Admetos deceived me.   690

SERVANT

Sometimes his hospitality goes too far.

HERAKLES

Was I supposed to join in your mourning an outsider?

SERVANT

O poor outsider!

HERAKLES

What's wrong here? Is there something I don't know?

SERVANT

Let it be. She was ours. These evils are ours.

HERAKLES

Don't sound like you're talking about any outsider.

SERVANT

No. Or I wouldn't be so distraught.

HERAKLES

You mean Admetos lied to me?

SERVANT

You came into the heart of our grief.
This is a house dressed in black.

700

HERAKLES

Who was it died?

SERVANT

Admetos' wife.

HERAKLES

What are you saying! And yet you entertained me?

SERVANT

He was ashamed to send you away.

HERAKLES

Headstrong man! What an insult to his wife.

SERVANT

To us all. We died with her.

HERAKLES

Well, I saw his eyes, his hair, the signs of mourning.
But he convinced me it was someone else who'd died.
He forced me to come in.
So there I was drinking, carousing, carrying on,   710
while the poor man suffered in the same house?
And you said nothing! This house is dark indeed.
Where is he burying her? Where can I find them?

SERVANT

Go straight that way on the Larisa road,
you will see the tomb just outside town.

HERAKLES

O heart, O hand of Herakles—
you have endured much!
Now prove what you're made of. Prove me a son of Zeus!

I must save dead Alkestis,

restore this house. 720

To Admetos I owe such a grace.

I shall go and keep watch for Death in his black robes.

He'll be drinking blood by the tomb.

If I lie in wait I can leap out, grab him,

get him in a grip he won't escape—until he sets the woman
    free.

And if I miss him there at his meal of blood

I'll go below

to the sunless kingdoms

and beg the king and queen. Believe me,

I shall bring Alkestis back. I'll put her in Admetos' hands. 730

He took me in when he was stricken.

He hid his loss, out of nobility, out of respect for me.

Who could do more than that? In all of Thessaly? In all of
    Greece?

He shall not say I was unworthy of it.

[exit Herakles by side entrance]

[exit Servant into house]

[enter Admetos by side entrance toward front door of palace]

ADMETOS

  I hate these doors! I hate the going in of doors!

    And empty rooms within.

      IO MOI MOI AIAI! *[cry of pain]*

      Where can I go? How can I stop? What should I say?

        Unlucky the mother who bore me.

        I envy the dead—I am in love with the dead. 740

How I long to dwell where they dwell
for I take no joy in the light of day
nor in setting my foot on the earth.
What a hostage death stole from me!

CHORUS
Go in, go in. Go on inside.

ADMETOS
AIAI! [*cry*]

CHORUS
Your suffering I see.

ADMETOS
E! E! [*cry*]

CHORUS
Your pain I understand.

ADMETOS
PHEU PHEU! [*cry*]   750

CHORUS
But it is of no avail.

ADMETOS
IO MOI MOI! [*cry*]

CHORUS
To never see her face again is what grief is.

ADMETOS

You reopen the wound in my mind.

What greater evil for a man than to lose his good wife?

I should never have wed.

Should never have lived with her here.

How I envy men who do not marry, have no children.

One soul each—that's enough to worry about!

Children struck down, bridal beds ravaged by death—   760

no one can bear it.

Why not just stay alone.

CHORUS

Fortune you cannot master.

ADMETOS

AIAI! [*cry*]

CHORUS

Nor put a limit to human pain.

ADMETOS

E! E! [*cry*]

CHORUS

Hard to bear but—

ADMETOS

PHEU PHEU! [*cry*]

CHORUS

you must. You are not the first

ADMETOS

IO MOI MOI! [*cry*]   770

CHORUS

to lose a wife.
Other mortals, other misfortunes.

ADMETOS

Sorrow is long
    when love has vanished underground.
        Why did you stop me throwing myself in her grave?
        I could have lain with her.
Death would have had two souls instead of one,
two steadfast souls to cross the lake of dread.

CHORUS

I know a man who lost a son,
    an only child, a perfect child.   780
        But still he bore it bravely,
            just an old man,
                without his dear one,
                    at the far edge of life.

ADMETOS

            O shape of my house, how can I enter you?
        How can I dwell where my luck has failed?
      So much inbetween.
    Once upon a time with torches of pine,
with wedding songs, I entered here,
    lifting my beloved wife by the hand,   790
        and the revel echoed around us,
            to bless Alkestis and me—

Good fathers, good families, good marriage! they said.
Now the song is no wedding song, the song is death.
Not white clothes but black clothes
send me in
to the empty desert of my bed.

CHORUS

On your lucky life,
on your untouched self,
this grief has come.   800
But you saved *you*!
A wife is dead, she left your love behind.
What's new in that?
Many men before now
has death detached
from wives.

ADMETOS

Friends! I count my wife luckier than me,
strange as that may seem.
No grief will ever touch her anymore.
She is stopped from pain. She has her glory.   810
While I, who should not be here, am loosened by fate
into anguish of living.
Too late I understand.
How shall I bear my entrance to this house?
Whom should I call out to, who will answer, where do I turn?
The desert inside laughs out at me.
When I see the empty bed
or the chair where she sat
or the dust on the floor,
when the children cry at my knees for their mother,   820

when the servants lament the lady they lost—
such is my house!
And outside—how can I face it?—
marriages everywhere, women everywhere, her friends
    everywhere.
Besides, there are people who hate me. They'll say,
"Look at him, the shame survivor!
Fed his wife to death in place of himself—is that a man?
He can bear anything but death!"
So they'll talk.
Friends, what good is living,   830
denounced and disaster-struck?

CHORUS (*fourth choral ode*)
                    I have searched in songs,
                    I have searched in books,
            I have speculated on the planets in the sky
                        and I find
                nothing stronger than Necessity.
                    There is no cure—
                        no Orphic lore,
        nor all the medications that Apollo gave the sons of Asklepios,
                to cut against pain and death.   840

                    Necessity, you alone need
                        no altar,
                        no image,
                        no sacrifice.
                Lady, I pray you, do not come at me.
                For whenever Zeus nods yes
                    you bring it to pass.

Your will can crush iron.
And your spirit is a cliff that knows not shame.

This goddess has you, Admetos, in her unbreakable bonds.   850
Endure it.
You will never recover the dead with weeping.
Even the children of gods fade off into shadow.
Dear to us in life she was,
dear to us in death,
your magnificent wife.

Let her grave not be counted as one of the ordinary kind
but valued as gods are,
reverenced by those who pass.
Someone will stop on the road and say: 860
"This woman died for her husband.
Now she is one of the blessed.
O lady, be gracious." So they will pray.

Admetos! look—here comes Herakles.

[enter Herakles with veiled woman from side entrance]

HERAKLES

Friends should speak freely to friends,
Admetos, not hold blame inside.
I stood by you in bad times.
I thought you valued me.
Yet you didn't bother explaining to me that the corpse in
    your house was your wife. You entertained me!
As if she were an outsider!   870

Alkestis

So I garlanded my head and drank to the gods
in a house that was grieving your dead.
I call this wrong. I call it wrong.
But it's not my wish to hurt you more.
Tell you why I've come back.
This woman—take her and keep her for me
until I return with the horses from Thrace.
If things don't go well there—I pray they do!—
I give her to you. She can serve in your house.
It was at considerable cost she came to my hands.   880
For I met some men setting up athletic games—open games,
good prizes—and I won her.
The lesser victors took home horses,
the greater—in wrestling and boxing—oxen.
The woman was a bonus.
It seemed a shame to waste.
So, as I say, she's in your charge.
She isn't stolen, I got her by fighting.
Some day you will thank me.

ADMETOS

Not because I wished to dishonor or embarrass you   890
did I hide my poor wife's fate.
But it would have added pain on top of pain to send you away.
Enough for me to weep my own loss.
As for this woman, I beg you, somehow, if you can,
let her go elsewhere.
You have many friends in Thessaly.
Don't remind me of my evils.
I couldn't bear to see her in the house.
Don't afflict me any more!
Besides, where in these rooms would a young woman stay?   900

For I see from her clothes she is young.
In the men's quarters? An innocent girl?
How will that work? Can men be restrained? I don't think so.
Or am I to put her in my dead wife's room?
Let her in there? How can I? Blame terrifies me—
blame from everyone in town,
when they see me jump into bed with a girl and betray my wife.
Blame from Alkestis herself—no! I must respect her.
I must be very *very* careful.
Woman, whoever you are, the truth is, you look like her!   910
You have the same shape.
Ah! [*cry of pain*] For gods' sake, take this woman away!
Don't beat me when I'm down!
I look on her and see my wife.
She makes my heart pound, my tears fall.
How bitter grief tastes!

CHORUS

What can I say?
One must take what the gods give.

HERAKLES

How I wish I had the power
to bring your wife out of darkness,   920
to give this grace to you.

ADMETOS

I know you wish that. But how?
The dead do not come back to light.

HERAKLES

Control yourself now.

ADMETOS

Easier said than done.

HERAKLES

What good does grief do?

ADMETOS

None. But longing compels me.

HERAKLES

To love the dead is endless tears.

ADMETOS

Her death destroys me, more than I can say.

HERAKLES

You lost a good woman, who will deny it?   930

ADMETOS

Life's pleasure is gone.

HERAKLES

Time will soften this. Your pain is new.

ADMETOS

If by time you mean death, then yes.

HERAKLES

A new woman, new marriage, is what you need.

ADMETOS

Silence! No. No.

HERAKLES

What? You won't marry, won't fill your bed?

ADMETOS

No woman will ever lie there.

HERAKLES

How will this help Alkestis? She's dead.

ADMETOS

Wherever she is, she deserves to be honored.

HERAKLES

Yes, yes, but people will call you a fool.   940

ADMETOS

So long as they don't call me bridegroom.

HERAKLES

I'm impressed. Your love is faithful.

ADMETOS

I would rather die than betray her now.

HERAKLES

Accept, then, this woman into your noble house.

ADMETOS

Oh no, I beg you, by Zeus your progenitor, no.

HERAKLES

You wrong me if you deny this.

ADMETOS

And if I do it, I cut my heart in two.

HERAKLES

Obey. Grace may arrive just when you need it.

ADMETOS

PHEU! [*cry of pain*]
How I wish you'd never won her from that contest.   950

HERAKLES

But I did. And in fact you win too.

ADMETOS

Beautifully said. Now let her go away.

HERAKLES

She will go, if need be. First look at her.

ADMETOS

She needs to go. Will you be angry?

HERAKLES

I have my reasons for insisting.

ADMETOS

You win. But I hate this.

HERAKLES

Someday you will praise me. For now, just obey.

ADMETOS

Bring her in.

HERAKLES

Oh I couldn't give her over to slaves.

ADMETOS

Then please take her yourself.   960

HERAKLES

Into your hands I will place her.

ADMETOS

No, I will not touch her!

HERAKLES

Put your trust in your own right hand.

ADMETOS

Herakles, you do violence to me.

HERAKLES

Courage. Reach out your hand. Touch her.

ADMETOS

It's like touching the Gorgon!

HERAKLES

Do you have her?

ADMETOS

I have her.

HERAKLES

Then keep her.
And forever say the son of Zeus was a noble guest.   970
Now look in her face. Does she not resemble your wife?
Put off your grief—rejoice!

ADMETOS

Gods! What can I say? This is beyond hope! Inconceivable!
Am I looking at my wife? My wife? Is it really Alkestis?
Not some trick sent by gods to mock me?

HERAKLES

No trick. This is your wife you're looking at.

ADMETOS

Not some phantasm from underground?

HERAKLES

Admetos, I am no ghost handler.

ADMETOS

But I buried her myself.

HERAKLES

Yes you did. No wonder you disbelieve.   980

ADMETOS

Am I to touch her, speak to her, as my own wife?

HERAKLES

Speak. You have all you desire.

ADMETOS

> O most beloved, O eyes I love, O face and form I never
> thought to see again!
> I have you! I have you here!

HERAKLES

> You have her. Let gods' envy stay away.

ADMETOS

> O noble son of highest Zeus,
> blessings upon you, may your father preserve you.
> You alone are my salvation.
> How did you send her back to the light?

HERAKLES

> I did battle with the god in charge.   990

ADMETOS

> With Death? Where?

HERAKLES

> By the tomb. I seized him from ambush.

ADMETOS

> Why does she stand so still?

HERAKLES

> She's not allowed to use her voice until three days have passed
> and she is purified of death.
> But take her in. And be a man of justice
> in the future. Reverence your guests.
> Now farewell. My labors call me.

ADMETOS

Wait, stay with us, be our guest.

HERAKLES

Another time. I have obligations.   1000

[exit Herakles by side entrance]

ADMETOS

Then fare you well. And do return.
To my townspeople and the whole territory I proclaim
dances and altars and sacrifice to celebrate our happiness.
Now we change our life!
The beauty of my luck I shall not deny.

[exit Admetos, Alkestis into central door]

CHORUS

Many are the shapes of things divine.
Many are the unexpected acts of gods.
What we imagined did not come to pass—
God found a way
to be surprising.   1010
That's how this went.

WHY I WROTE TWO PLAYS ABOUT PHAIDRA

by Euripides[1]

Your faces, I don't understand them. At night I stand at the back of the theater. I watch you suck in sex, death, devastation, hour after hour in a weird kind of unresisting infant heat, then for no reason you cool, flicker out. I guess *for no reason* is an arrogant thing to say. For no reason I can name is what I mean. It was a few years ago now I gave you a woman, a real mouthful of salt and you like salt. Her story, Phaidra's story, that old story, came in as a free wave and crashed on your beach. I don't understand, I could never have predicted, your hatred of this woman. It's true she fell in love with someone wrong for her but half the heroines of your literature do that, Helen, Echo, Io, Agave, all of them. Phaidra's love was for her stepson, and it excited you badly, maybe not the incest so much as a question of property rights—ditch the old man, marry the son, keep the estate. Truth is often, in some degree, economic. Which isn't to say her passion for Hippolytos was fake. Women learn to veil things. Who likes to look straight at real passion? Looks can kill. I would call "feminine" this talent for veiling a truth in a truth. As if truths were skins of one

---

1. The Athenian tragedian Euripides (c. 484–c. 406 BC) appears to have made two attempts to compose a tragedy on the myth of Phaidra and her disastrous infatuation with her stepson Hippolytos. We have one complete tragedy called *Hippolytos* (produced 428 BC) and some fragments of an earlier version called *Hippolytos Veiled* (date of production uncertain). The earlier version was a flop. It seems to have offended audiences by portraying Phaidra as a bold sexual predator who confronts Hippolytos directly with her desire. The later version reimagines Phaidra and her virtue: she agonizes about keeping her lust a secret; is shocked to find her feelings betrayed to Hippolytos by an old Nurse; recoils from addressing the young man face-to-face; overhears him saying bad things about her and hangs herself offstage.

another and the ability to move, hunt, negotiate among them was a way of finessing the terms of the world in which we find ourselves. Skin game, so to speak. Phaidra played the skin game disastrously, sadly, but you didn't see her as sad. You saw her white hot—an incision into some other layer of life, some core.

Phaidra didn't care about you. She didn't care about property. She didn't care about the game. She didn't even really care about Hippolytos—but she cared (was this what you saw?) about the core. Eros itself. She knew that was real. And knew she would fail it. Even as she wrapped its white heat in economic arguments, royal bed, palace power, his, his, his, this! this! this! ultimate sexual casino of stuff and honor and winning, she saw her own apostasy. Too many truths in between and Hippolytos just one of them, the lovely, careless, wry boy. And maybe that was the reason she killed herself in the end—realizing the object of her heart's desire could become just one more skin in the endless process of paring compromise off compromise, bid from bid, seduction from seduction, turned her against her own life. There was shame in her but not the kind you wanted to see, not woman's modesty. She was ashamed *at the core.* Ashamed to have veiled Hippolytos in himself. What do we desire when we desire other people? Not them. Something else. Phaidra touched it. You hated her for that.

Hippolytos Veiled was what I called my first attempt to write a play about Phaidra. This play did not succeed. It disappointed you. You thought the title meant Hippolytos would be shown in scenes of deep revulsion, veiling his head before the wantonness of the mother. You thought the shame was his, the veil was his, the love was wrong in some simple way that you could grasp before the first choral song. But we all burned our hands on that Phaidra, didn't we? It was her shame that ate the play. And her shame wasn't simple. It pullulated and turned on itself and stank at the bottom of the pit of the question of desire—what is the question of desire? I don't know. Something about its presumption to exist in human forms. Human forms are puny. Desire is vast. Vast, absolute and oddly *general.* A big general liquid washing through the universe, filling puny vessels here and there as it were arbitrarily, however it lights on them, swamping some, splitting others, casually ruinous—an "Aphrodite" as we call that throw of the dice that comes up nine and changes the game. Doesn't win the game, just changes it.

But to continue. You didn't like Phaidra so I started over. Wrote another play, it took years. Called this one *Hippolytos,* no veil. To get rid of the veil I had to pull shame out of the inside of Phaidra and spread it on all her surfaces, on all the surfaces of the play, like a single hurt color. Shame is many things. In *Hippolytos,* shame is what the boy worships as a goddess in the form of Artemis, a pure uncut watergreen shame that reminds him of his own virginity. Shame is also the blush that dyes Phaidra so hot she cannot live in the same body with it. Odd that this virtue, also a vice, is one they share without seeing how. "Shame lives on the eyelids" according to an old Greek proverb.[2] I guess this means it makes you cast your eyes down, or that it blinds you. Both Phaidra and Hippolytos act in a blindness as they grapple, deflect and slide past one another into death. There is no moment of confrontation or truth between the two. They never exchange a touch, word or glance. Shame segregates them so effectively, they live and die within earshot of one another, out of reach on the same stage. Pathos like that could win me first prize this time, don't you think? But pathos isn't the reason I wrote this play.

In general I like women. I like glossing around in women's language, so different from men's. But this one seized me as no other

2. Stobaeus, *Florilegium* 4.230.

character ever had—that first Phaidra, the pure chainsmoking nihilism of her, pacing the cage of her own clarity. What rushed through her speech wasn't fuss about mirrors and chastity. Only a fool would have asked her for a *moral position*. Her people feared her. Her own spirit feared her. You feared her.

So, Phaidra—a work in motion, surpassing her, surpassing itself—disappears again and again into *Phaidra* after *Phaidra*, but she is not gone, her disappearance in fact reverberates everywhere in this so-called second version. I wrote it to show how that feels. Phaidraless world. Her great soul withdrawn, the story goes through its tricks in a weak voltage of vicious reactions and bad piety, which I hope will amuse you but this fact remains, there is no shock in it anywhere except Aphrodite. Aphrodite is pure shock. When she comes onstage in the prologue and tells you about a few simple stitches she is going to take in the lives of Phaidra, Hippolytos and Theseus, you feel the salt of absolute cruelty sting your face. That needle flashes in and out of living skulls. I guess by the time I came to write the prologue (I usually write the prologue last) I had pretty much given up on saving Phaidra, the real one. But there is a residue of her gone down into Aphrodite's anger. It is sexual anger. Or is all anger sexual? Remember (if you saw the first play) the advice Phaidra gives to her pale groaning husband when he confronts her about the boy:

Phaidra: Instead of fire—another fire,
> *not just a drop of cunt sweat!* is what we women are—
> you cannot fight it! [3]

3. Euripides, fragment of *Hippolytos Veiled*.

TITLES IN SERIES

For a list of titles, visit www.nyrb.com or write to:
Catalog Requests, NYRB, 435 Hudson Street, New York, NY 10014